THE GOSPEL OF HEALING

THE
GOSPEL OF
HEALING

A.B. SIMPSON

CHRISTIAN PUBLICATIONS
CAMP HILL, PENNSYLVANIA

CHRISTIAN PUBLICATIONS, INC.
3825 Hartzdale Drive, Camp Hill, PA 17011
www.christianpublications.com

Faithful, biblical publishing since 1883

The Gospel of Healing
ISBN: 0-87509-376-0
LOC Control Number: 86-70736
© 1994 by Christian Publications

Unless otherwise indicated
Scripture taken from the
Holy Bible: King James Version

CONTENTS

INTRODUCTION

The *Gospel of Healing* was the first of Albert B. Simpson's more than 100 books. Chapters 1-3 originally appeared in 1883 as articles in his magazine, *The Word, The Work and The World*. In 1885 the next three appeared in the same publication. Prior to June 1885, some or all of these articles were put together in the first edition of *The Gospel of Healing*. (Unfortunately, no copies of that first edition are known to be in existence.)

The book passed through many editions, chapters 7 and 8 being added by 1888. That edition was revised in 1915, in Simpson's 72nd year. Very little was deleted or altered.

Unlike many of Simpson's books, *The Gospel of Healing* began as a written document rather than a collection of spoken sermons. Although the views represent Simpson's earliest perceptions of the truth of divine healing, throughout his lifetime he saw no necessity to retract or alter his early views. Divine healing was a frequent theme in all of his publications and sermons. In none of them are there views at variance with or in addition to what is expressed in *The Gospel of Healing*.

In January 1918, at age 74, Dr. Simpson suffered a stroke. He and Mrs. Simpson went to Clifton Springs, New York, for rest and recuperation, hopeful that he might resume an active ministry. But he did not experience the recovery he desired.

Although he personally wanted the Lord to prolong his ministry, he finally yielded to his own teaching that divine healing has a terminal point, that divine health was God's promise to His children until He chose to conclude their ministry. Although weakened in body, Simpson preached occasionally, counseled with his fellow ministers, attended some meetings and prayed alone and with his friends in rich communion and intercession. Apparently he suffered no pain during this period. On October 30, 1919, he slipped quietly from his earthly tabernacle to enter peaceably into the presence of the Lord.

A century after they were first set down in writing, Simpson's views of divine healing may seem to you unnecessary, even impractical. Medical science has advanced rapidly; doctors can prescribe remedies to end most of our illnesses. We can be thankful that humankind has such ready help. But this fact does not negate the truth of divine healing. Christ the Healer does not require the assistance of medical skills.

In this day, Simpson refused to impose his views of healing on others. He taught the truth as he saw it and experienced it. He only desired that his auditors or readers would understand the teaching, then examine the truth for themselves. If and when they were personally convinced and ready in heart and mind to commit themselves irrevocably to the Lord for His divine life, then and only then did Simpson consider them ready to be anointed and prayed for.

In publishing this book, Simpson simply wished to expose his readers to the truth as he perceived it. That exposure is your privilege as you read. Consider the teaching carefully. Ask the Holy Spirit to "guide you into all truth" (John 16:13). God declares, "I am the LORD, I change not" (Malachi 3:6). "Jesus Christ [is] the same yesterday, and today, and for ever" (Hebrews 13:8).

A final word. Simpson published periodicals for more than 35 years. As one reads through these thousands of pages, the meetings, teaching and testimonies devoted to divine healing are both prominent and impressive. The Lord gave to Simpson a large ministry of healing, probably larger than to any other individual from the mid-19th century into the early 20th.

Yet Simpson refused to allow divine healing to become a major feature at his church or at his many city conventions and summer camp meetings. A deeper Christian life, the salvation of sinners and a commitment to worldwide evangelization were far more important to him.

Simpson shied away from any ministry that could attract attention to himself. His single interest was to instruct people in "the way of the Lord," to promote in them faith and trust. He wanted seekers to fix their eyes on Jesus alone. From the resurrected Jesus—not from any man— flowed divine life and health.

To grasp Simpson's view is what this book is all about.

John S. Sawin
Simpson Archivist
1986

PREFACE

The first half of this volume has been issued in many successive editions as a series of tracts on the gospel of healing. The testimony of many persons that the tracts have been greatly blessed of God, and the desire often expressed to have them in permanent form, have induced the author to reissue them in a book with the addition of several fresh chapters. It is hoped that this simple volume may now be found to be a compact and more useful channel of scriptural instruction upon this important subject.

The views expressed have been carefully weighed in the balance of the divine Word. They have been confirmed by much experience and careful observation.

The importance of this subject and the emphatic way in which God's Holy Spirit is pressing it upon the attention of His people demand for it the most careful and thorough scriptural study. Effectual faith can only come through thorough conviction.

In spite of the cold and conservative and sometimes scornful unbelief of many, this doctrine is becoming one of the touchstones of character and spiritual life.

It is revolutionizing, by a deep, quiet and divine movement, the whole Christian life of thousands. It has a profound bearing upon the spiritual life. No one can truly receive it without becoming a holier and more useful Christian.

It is most important that it should be ever held in its true place in relation to the other parts of the gospel. It is not the whole gospel, or perhaps the chief part of it, but it is a part, and in its due relationship to the whole it will prove to be, like the gospel itself, "the power of God . . . to every one that believeth."

Albert B. Simpson

CHAPTER
1

The Scriptural Foundation

Man has a twofold nature. He is both a material and a spiritual being. And both natures have been equally affected by the Fall. His body is exposed to disease; his soul is corrupted by sin. How blessed, therefore, to find that the complete scheme of redemption includes both natures. It provides for the restoration of physical as well as the renovation of spiritual life!

The Redeemer appears among men with His hands stretched out to our misery and need, offering both salvation and healing. He offers Himself to us as a Savior to the uttermost; His indwelling Spirit, the life of our spirit; His resurrection body, the life of our mortal flesh.

Jesus begins His ministry by healing all who have need of healing; He closes it by making full atonement for our sin on the cross. Then, on the other side of the open tomb, He passes into heaven, leaving the double commission for "all nations" and "alway, even unto the end of the world" (Matthew 28:19–20).

He says, "Go ye into all the world, and preach the gospel to every creature. He that believeth and is baptized shall be saved; but he that believeth not shall be damned. And these signs shall follow them that believe; In my name shall they cast out devils; . . . they shall lay hands on the sick, and they shall recover" (Mark 16:15–18).

This was "the faith . . . once delivered unto the saints" (Jude 3). What has become of it? Why is it not still universally taught and realized? Did it disappear with the apostolic age? Was it withdrawn when Peter, Paul and John were removed? By no means! It remained in the church for centuries and only disappeared gradually in the church's growing worldliness, corruption, formalism and unbelief.

With a reviving faith, with a deepening spiritual life, with a more marked and scriptural recognition of the Holy Spirit and the living Christ and with the nearer approach of the returning Master Himself, this blessed gospel of physical redemption is beginning to be restored to its ancient place. The church is slowly learning to reclaim what she never should have lost. But along with this there is also manifested such a spirit of conservative unbelief and cold, traditional theological rationalism as to make it necessary that we should "earnestly contend for the faith which was once delivered unto the saints."

Faith Must Rest on the Word

First, we must be sure of our scriptural foundations. Faith must always rest on the divine Word. The most important element in the "prayer of faith" is a full and firm persuasion that the healing of disease by simple faith in God is a part of the gospel and a doctrine of the Scriptures.

The earliest promise of healing is in Exodus 15:25–26: "There he made for them a statute and an ordinance, and there he proved them, and said, If thou wilt diligently hearken to the voice of the LORD thy God, and wilt do that which is right in his sight, and wilt give ear to his commandments, and keep all his statutes, I will put none of these diseases upon thee, which I have brought upon the Egyptians: for I am the LORD that healeth thee."

The place of this promise is most marked. It is at the very outset of Israel's journey from Egypt, like Christ's healing of disease at the opening of His ministry.

It comes immediately after Israel passed through the Red Sea. This event is distinctly typical of our redemption, and the journey of the Israelites in the wilderness is typical of our pilgrimage: "These things happened unto them for ensamples: and they are written for our admonition, upon whom the ends of the world are come" (1 Corinthians 10:11).

This promise, therefore, becomes ours as the redeemed people of God. And God meets us at the very threshold of our pilgrimage with the covenant of healing. He declares that, as we walk in holy and loving obedience, we shall be kept from sickness, which belongs to the old life of bondage we have left behind us forever.

Sickness belongs to the Egyptians, not to the people of God. And only as we return spiritually to Egypt do we return to its malarias and perils. This is not only a promise; it is "a statute and an ordinance." And so, corresponding to this ancient statute, the Lord Jesus has left for us in James 5:14 a distinct ordinance of healing in His name, as sacred and binding as any of the ordinances of the gospel.

In Psalm 105:37 we read of the actual fulfillment of that promise: "He brought them forth also with silver and gold: and there was not one feeble person among their tribes." Although they did not fulfill their part in the covenant, God kept His word. And so, although our faith and obedience are often defective, if Christ is our surety and if our faith will claim His merits and His name, we too shall see the promise fulfilled.

Satan the Source

The story of Job is one of the oldest records of history. It gives us a view of the source from which sickness came—in this case, Satan (Job 1–2). It also reveals the course of action that brings healing—that is, taking the place of humble self-judgment at the mercy seat. If ever a sickroom was unveiled, it was that of the man of Uz. But we see no physician there, no human remedy, only a looking unto God as his Avenger. And when Job renounces his self-righteousness and self-vindication and takes the place where God is seeking to bring him—that of self-renunciation and humility—he is healed.

The psalms of David are a record of many afflictions. But God is always the deliverer, and God alone: "Bless the LORD, O my soul, and forget not all his benefits: who forgiveth all thine iniquities; who healeth all thy diseases" (Psalm 103:2–3). We see no human hand. The psalmist looks to heaven as directly for healing as he does for pardon, and in the same breath he cries: "Who forgiveth all thine iniquities; who healeth all thy diseases." It is a complete healing—*all* his diseases—as universal and lasting as the forgiveness of his sins. And how glorious and entire that was is evident enough: "As far as the east is from the west, so far hath he removed our transgressions from us" (103:12). But here, as in the case of Job, there is an intimate connection between sickness and sin, and both must be healed together.

Asa was a king who had begun his reign by an act of simple, implicit trust in God when human resources utterly failed him. By that trust he won one of the most glorious victories of history (2 Chronicles 14:9–12). But success corrupted him. It taught him to value too highly the arm of flesh. In his next great crisis, Asa formed an alliance with Syria and lost the help of God

(16:7–8). He refused to take warning from the prophet and rushed on to the climax of his earthly confidence.

Asa became sick. Here was a greater foe than the Ethiopians, but again he turned to man: "And Asa in the thirty and ninth year of his reign was diseased in his feet, until his disease was exceeding great: yet in his disease he sought not to the LORD, but to the physicians" (16:12). The outcome could not be more sad or sarcastic: "And Asa slept with his fathers" (16:13).

The Old Testament Evangel

It was Isaiah who delivered the great evangelical vision, the gospel in the Old Testament, the very mirror of the coming Redeemer. And at the front of his prophetic message, prefaced by a great Amen—the only "surely" in the chapter—is the promise of healing: "Surely he hath borne our griefs, and carried our sorrows . . . and with his stripes we are healed" (Isaiah 53:4–5). It is the strongest possible statement of complete redemption from pain and sickness by Christ's life and death. And these are the very words Matthew quotes afterward, under the inspired guidance of the Holy Spirit (Matthew 8:17), as the explanation of Jesus' universal works of healing.

Our English version of Isaiah does only imperfect justice to the force of the original. The translation in Matthew is much better: "Himself took our infirmities, and bare our sicknesses." A literal translation of Isaiah would be: "Surely he hath borne away our sicknesses and carried away our pains."

Any person who will refer to such a familiar commentary as that of Albert Barnes on Isaiah, or to any other Hebrew authority, will see that the two words denote respectively *sickness* and *pain*. And the words for "bear" and "carry" denote not mere sympathy but actual substitution and the utter removal of the thing borne.

Therefore, as Jesus Christ has borne our sins, He has also borne away and carried off our sicknesses, yes, and even our pains. Abiding in Him, we may be fully delivered from both sickness and pain. Thus "by his stripes we are healed." Blessed and glorious gospel! Blessed and glorious Burden-Bearer!

And so the ancient prophet beholds in vision the Redeemer coming first as a great Physician and then hanging on the cross as a great Sacrifice. The evangelists have also described Him so. For three years He was the great Healer, and then for six hours of shame and agony He was the dying Lamb.

Jesus Fulfills Prophecy

Matthew, inspired by God, quotes Isaiah 53:4–5 as the reason why Jesus healed all who were sick: "He . . . healed all that were sick: that it might be fulfilled which was spoken by Esaias the prophet, saying, Himself took our infirmities, and bare our sicknesses" (Matthew 8:16–17).

It was not that Jesus might give His enemies a

vindication of His Deity, but that He might fulfill the character presented of Him in ancient prophecy. Had He not done so, He would not have been true to His own character. If He did not still do so, He would not be "Jesus Christ the same yesterday, and to day, and for ever" (Hebrews 13:8). These healings were not occasional but continual, not exceptional but universal. Jesus never turned any away. "He . . . healed all that were sick." "As many as touched him were made whole." He is still the same.

This was the work of Jesus' life, and God would not have us forget that His Son spent more than three years in deeds of power and love before He went up to Calvary to die. We need that living Christ quite as much as we need Christ crucified. The Levitical types included the meal offering as much as the sin offering. And suffering humanity needs to feed upon the great loving Heart of Galilee and Bethany as much as on the Lamb of Calvary.

It would take entirely too long to examine in detail the countless records of Jesus' healing power and grace. He cured the leper, the lame, the blind, the paralytic, the impotent, the fever-stricken—all who "had need of healing." He linked sickness often with sin and forgave before He spoke the restoring word. He required their own personal touch of appropriating faith and bade them take the healing by rising up and carrying their beds.

His healing went far beyond His own immediate presence to reach and save the centurion's servant and the nobleman's son. How often He reproved the least question of His willingness to help and threw the responsibility of man's suffering on his own unbelief.

These and many more such lessons crowd every page of the Master's life and reveal to us the secret of claiming His healing power. What right has anyone to explain these miracles as mere types of spiritual healing and not as specimens of what He still is ready to do for all who trust Him? Such was Jesus of Nazareth.

Jesus Empowers Others to Heal

But was this blessed power to die with Jesus at Calvary? Jesus does not so indicate. "Verily, verily, I say unto you, He that believeth on me, the works that I do shall he do also; and greater works than these shall he do; because I go unto my Father" (John 14:12). Jesus makes it emphatic—"verily, verily"—as if He knew it was something mankind was sure to doubt. It is no use to tell us that this meant that the church after Pentecost was to have greater spiritual power and do greater spiritual works by the Holy Spirit than Jesus Himself did, inasmuch as the conversion of the soul is a greater work than the healing of the body. Jesus says, "The works that I do shall he do also," as well as the "greater works than these." That is, Jesus' followers are to do the same works that He Himself did and greater also.

Even during His life on earth Jesus sent out the

12 apostles. Then He sent out the 70 as forerunners of the whole host of the Christian eldership (for the 70 were in effect the first elders of the Christian age, corresponding to the 70 elders of Moses' time) with full power to heal. And when Jesus was about to leave the world, He left on record both these commissions in the most unmistakable terms.

A Twofold Commission

> *Go ye into all the world, and preach the gospel to every creature. He that believeth and is baptized shall be saved; but he that believeth not shall be damned. And these signs shall follow them that believe; In my name shall they cast out devils; they shall speak with new tongues; They shall take up serpents; and if they drink any deadly thing, it shall not hurt them; they shall lay hands on the sick, and they shall recover. (Mark 16:15–18)*

Here is the commission of the twofold gospel given to them and the assurance of Christ's presence and unchanging power. What right have we to preach one part of the gospel without the other? What right have we to hold back any of God's grace from a perishing world? What right have we to go to unbelievers and demand their acceptance of our salvation message without these signs following? What right have we to explain their absence from our ministry by trying to eliminate them from God's Word or to consign them to an obsolete past?

Christ promised the signs, and they followed as long as Christians continued to believe and expect them. It is important to observe Young's translation of verse 17: "Signs shall follow them that believe these things." The signs shall correspond to the extent of their faith.

By such mighty "signs and wonders" the church was established in Jerusalem, Samaria and unto the uttermost parts of the earth. The unbelief of the world needs these signs today as much as in the apostolic times. During the apostolic age these manifestations of healing power were by no means confined to the apostles. Philip and Stephen were as gloriously used as Peter and John.

In First Corinthians 12:9, "the gifts of healing" are spoken of as widely diffused and universally understood among the endowments of the church. But the apostolic age was soon to close; were the gifts to be continued, and if so, by whom? By what limitation was the church to be preserved from fanaticism and presumption? By what commission was healing to be perpetuated to the end of time and placed within the reach of all God's suffering saints?

The answer is in James 5:14-15, to which we turn again with deep interest: "Is any sick among you? let him call for the elders of the church; and let them pray over him, anointing him with oil in the name of the Lord: and the prayer of faith shall save the sick, and the Lord shall raise him up; and if he have committed sins, they shall be forgiven him."

Notice first who gives this commission. It is James—James, who had authority to say, in summing up the decrees of the council at Jerusalem, "My sentence is . . ." He is the man who is named first by Paul himself among the pillars of the church (see Galatians 2:9).

Observe to whom this power is committed. Not to the apostles, who are now passing away; not to men and women of rare gifts or difficult to contact. It was given to the elders—the men most likely to be within reach of every sufferer, the men who are to continue till the end of the age.

Notice the time at which this commission is given. It was not at the beginning, but at the close of the apostolic age. It was not for that generation, but for the one that was just rising and all the succeeding ages. Indeed, these New Testament letters were not widely circulated in their own time, but were mainly designed "for our admonition, upon whom the ends of the world are come."

Again, observe the nature of the ordinance enjoined. It is "the prayer of faith" and the "anointing . . . with oil in the name of the Lord." This was not a medical anointing, for it was not to be applied by a physician, but by an elder. It must, naturally, be the same anointing we read of in connection with the healing of disease by the apostles (for instance, Mark 6:13).

Any other interpretation would be strained and contrary to the obvious meaning of the custom as our Lord and His apostles observed it. In the absence of any explanation to the contrary, we are bound to believe that it was the same—a symbolic religious ordinance expressive of the power of the Holy Spirit, whose peculiar emblem is oil.

The Greek Orthodox church still retains the ordinance, but the Roman Catholic church has changed it into a mournful preparation for death. It is a beautiful symbol of the divine Spirit of life taking possession of the human body and breathing into it God's vital energy.

Divine Healing Is a Command

Divine healing ceases to be a mere privilege. It is the divine prescription for disease, and no obedient Christian can safely ignore it. Any other method of dealing with sickness is unauthorized. This is God's plan. This makes faith simple and easy. We have only to obey in childlike confidence; God will fulfill.

Once more, we must not overlook the connection of sickness with sin. There is here the suggestion that the trial has been a divine chastening and requires self-judgment, penitence and pardon. There is the blessed assurance that both pardon and healing may be claimed together in His name.

If more were needed than the testimony of James, then John, the last of the apostles and the one who best knew the Master's heart, has left a tender prayer: "Beloved, I wish [pray] above all things that thou mayest prosper and be in health, even as thy soul prospereth" (3 John 2). By this prayer we may know our Father's gentle concern for our health as well as for our souls. When God breathes such a prayer for us, we need not fear to claim it for ourselves. But as we do, we must not forget that our health will be even as our soul prospers.

In Ephesians 5:30 we note a union between our body and the risen body of the Lord Jesus Christ: "We are members of his body, of his flesh, and of his bones." We have the right to claim for our mortal frame the vital energy of Christ's perfect life. He has given His life for us, and it is all-sufficient.

"If the Spirit of him that raised up Jesus from the dead dwell in you, he that raised up Christ from the dead shall also quicken your mortal bodies by his Spirit that dwelleth in you" (Romans 8:11). This promise cannot refer to the future resurrection. That resurrection will be by the "voice of the Son of God" (John 5:25), not the Holy Spirit. This is a present dwelling in and a quickening by the Spirit. And it is a quickening of the "mortal body," not the soul.

What can this be but physical restoration? The physical restoration is the direct work of the Holy Spirit, and only they who know the indwelling of the divine Spirit can receive it. It was the Spirit of God who wrought the miracles of Jesus Christ on earth (Matthew 12:28). And if we have the same Spirit dwelling in us, we shall experience the same works.

Not Simply Healing but Health

Paul expressed his physical experience this way: "Always bearing about in the body the dying of the Lord Jesus, that the life also of Jesus might be made manifest in our body. For we which live are alway delivered unto death for Jesus' sake, that the life also of Jesus might be made manifest in our mortal flesh" (2 Corinthians 4:10–11).

Paul knew constant peril, infirmity and physical suffering—probably by persecution and even violence. But it came in order that the healing, restoring and sustaining power and life of Jesus might be the more constantly manifest in his very body. And this for the encouragement of suffering saints—"for your sakes" (4:15). His life was a constant miracle that it might be to all persons a pledge and monument of the promise made to him for all who might thereafter suffer. This life, he tells us, was "renewed day by day" (4:16). The healing power of Christ is dependent on our continual abiding in Him and, like all God's gifts, is renewed day by day.

Christ did not say, "I *will be* with you alway." That would have suggested a break. He said, "I *am*"—an unchanging now, a presence never withdrawn, a love, a nearness, a power to heal and save as constant and as free as ever, even unto the end of the world. "Jesus Christ the same yesterday, and to day, and for ever."

Thus have we traced the teachings of the Holy Scriptures from Exodus to Patmos. We have seen

God giving His people the ordinance of healing at the very outset of their pilgrimage. We have seen it illustrated in the ancient dispensation in the sufferings of Job, the songs of David and the sad death of Asa. We have seen Isaiah's prophetic vision of the coming Healer. We have seen the Son of Man coming to fulfill that picture to the letter; we have heard Him tell His weeping disciples of His unchanging presence with them. We have seen Him transmit His healing power to their hands. And we have seen those followers hand down this gospel of healing to us and to the church of God until the latest ages of time.

What more evidence can we ask? What else can we do but believe, rejoice, receive and proclaim this great salvation to a sick and sinking world?

CHAPTER
2

Principles of
Divine Healing

There are certain principles underlying the teachings of the Holy Scriptures with respect to healing that are important to understand. When rightly comprehended, they are most helpful to intelligent faith.

The causes of disease and suffering are distinctly traced to the Fall and the sinful state of man. If sickness were part of the natural constitution of things, then we might meet it wholly on natural grounds and by natural means. But if it be part of the curse of sin, it must have its true remedy in the great Redemption. That sickness is the result of the Fall and one of the fruits of sin, no one can surely question. Death, we are told, has passed upon all, for all have sinned, and the greater includes the less.

Sickness is named among the curses that God

was to send for Israel's sin (Deuteronomy 28:58–61). Again, sickness is distinctly connected with Satan's personal agency. He was the direct instrument of Job's suffering; and our Lord definitely attributed the diseases of His time directly to satanic power. It was Satan who bound the paralyzed woman "these eighteen years." It was demonic influence that held and crushed the bodies and souls of those Christ delivered. If sickness is the result of a spirit agency, it is most evident that it must be met and counteracted by a higher spiritual force and not by mere natural treatment.

And on the supposition that sickness is a divine discipline and chastening, it is still more evident that its removal must come not through mechanical or medical appliances, but through spiritual channels. It would be both ridiculous and vain for the arm of man to presume to wrest the chastening rod from the Father's hand by physical force or skill. The only way to avert God's stroke is to submit the spirit in penitence to His will and seek in humility and faith His forgiveness and relief.

From whatever side we look at disease, it becomes evident that its remedy must be found in God alone and the gospel of redemption.

Since disease is the result of the Fall, we may expect it to be embraced in the provisions of redemption. Therefore, we naturally will look for some intimation of a remedy in the preparatory dispensation to Christ's coming and the preaching of the gospel.

We are not disappointed. The great principle that God's care and providence embrace the temporal and physical as well as the spiritual needs of His people runs all through the Old Testament. Distinct provision for divine healing is made in all the ordinances of Moses. And the prophetic picture of the coming Deliverer is that of a great Physician as well as a glorious King and gracious Savior.

The healing of Abimelech, Miriam, Job, Naaman and Hezekiah; the case of the leper; the incident of the brazen serpent; the statute at Marah; the blessings and curses at Ebal and Gerizim; the terrible rebuke of Asa; the message of Psalm 103 and Chapter 53 of Isaiah—all leave the testimony of the Old Testament clear that the redemption of the body was the divine prerogative and purpose.

The Ministry of Christ

The personal ministry of Jesus Christ is the next great stage in the development of the principles of divine healing. In Christ's life on earth, we see a complete vision of what Christianity should be. From Jesus' words and works, we may surely gather the full plan of redemption. And what was the testimony of His life to physical healing? He went about their cities healing all manner of sickness and disease among the people. He healed all who had need of healing, "that it might be fulfilled which was spoken by Esaias the prophet, saying, Himself took our infirmities, and bare our sicknesses" (Matthew 8:17).

This was not an occasional incident. It was a chief part of Jesus' ministry. He began His work by healing the sick. He continued to heal to the close of His life. He healed on all occasions and in a great variety of cases. He healed without leaving any doubt or question of His will. He distinctly said to the doubting leper, "I will." He was only grieved when people hesitated to trust Him fully.

In all this Jesus was unfolding the real purpose of His great redemption and revealing His own unchanging character and love. He is still "the same yesterday, and to day, and for ever" (Hebrews 13:8). Surely we have a principle to rest our faith on as secure as the Rock of Ages.

Healing Is Centered in the Atonement

Redemption finds its center in the cross of our Lord Jesus Christ. There we must look for the fundamental principle of divine healing, which rests on Jesus' atoning sacrifice. This necessarily follows from the first principle we have stated: If sickness is the result of the Fall, it must be included in the atonement of Christ, which reaches as "far as the curse is found."

Peter states of Christ, "his own self bare our sins in his own body on the tree, . . . by whose stripes ye were healed" (1 Peter 2:24). In His own body He has borne all our bodily liabilities for sin, and our bodies are set free. In that one cruel "stripe" of His—for the word is singular—was summed up all the aches and pains of a suffering world. There is no longer need that we should suffer what Christ has sufficiently borne. Thus our healing becomes a great redemption right that we simply claim as our purchased inheritance through the blood of Christ's cross.

Beyond the Cross

But there is something higher even than the cross. It is the resurrection of our Lord. There the gospel of healing finds the fountain of its deepest life. The death of Christ destroys sin— the root of sickness. But it is the life of Jesus that supplies the source of health and life for our redeemed bodies. The body of Christ is the living fountain of all our vital strength. He who came forth from Joseph's tomb with the new physical life of the resurrection is the Head of His people for life and immortality.

Not for Himself alone did Jesus receive the power of an endless life. He received it as our life. God "gave him to be the head over all things to the church, which is his body" (Ephesians 1:22– 23). "We are members of his body, of his flesh, and of his bones" (5:30). The risen and ascended Christ is the fountain of our strength and life. We eat His flesh and drink His blood. He dwells in us and we in Him. As He lives in the Father, so he who eats Him shall live by Him. This is the great, vital, precious principle of physical healing in the name of Jesus. It is "the life also of Jesus . . . made manifest in our mortal flesh" (2 Corinthians 4:11).

Healing Is New Life

It follows that this life must be wholly a new life. The death and resurrection of the Lord Jesus have made an infinite gulf between the present and the past of every redeemed person. Henceforth, "if any man be in Christ, he is a new creature: old things are passed away; behold, all things are become new" (2 Corinthians 5:17). The death of Jesus has slain our old self. The life of Jesus is the spring of our new life.

This is true also of our physical life. God does not restore the old natural strength. He does not build up our former constitution. We must let go all the old dependencies. Our natural strength may fail. The life of Jesus is a strength that "out of weakness [is] made strong." It is a life that has no resources to start with. Creation-like, it is made out of nothing; resurrection-like, it comes out of the tomb and the failure of all previous hope and means.

This principle is of immense importance in the practical experience of healing. So long as we look for healing in the old natural life, we shall be disappointed. But when we cease to put confidence in the flesh and look only to Christ and His supernatural life in us for our strength of body as well as spirit, we shall find that we "can do all things through Christ which strengtheneth [us]."

It follows from this that the physical redemption that Christ brings is not merely healing but also life. It is not the readjustment of our life on the old basis, leaving it to go like a machine upon the natural plane. It is the imparting of a new kind of life and strength; therefore, it is as fully within the reach of people in health as those who are diseased. It is simply a higher kind of life— the turning of life's water into His heavenly wine.

It is only kept by constant abiding in Jesus and receiving from Him. It is not a permanent deposit but a constant dependence, a renewing of the inward man day by day. It is a strength that comes only as we need it and continues only while we dwell in Him.

A Sacred Life

Such a life is a very sacred thing. It gives a peculiar sanctity to every look, tone, act and movement of the body. We are living on the life of God, and we must live like Him and for Him. A body thus divinely quickened adds power to the soul and to all the service of the Christian life. Words spoken in this divine energy and works done through the life of God will be clothed with a positive effectiveness which must make others feel that our bodies as well as our spirits are indeed the very temple of the holy God.

The great Agent in bringing this new life into our life is the Holy Spirit. The redemption work of the Lord Jesus is not completed without His blessed ministry. Not as a visible physical presence does the Savior of sinners and of the diseased now meet the sick and halt and blind, but through the Spirit. All the old physical power is there. All the ancient results upon the suffering frame are produced, but the approach is spiritual, not physical.

The presence of Christ must be brought to our consciousness. But the contact of our need with His life must come through the Holy Spirit. So Mary had to learn in the very first moment of the resurrection. "Touch me not . . . I ascend." Thus, henceforth, must she know Him as the Ascended One. So Paul had ceased to know Christ Jesus "after the flesh."

Our Lord, when speaking to the disciples at Capernaum of the living Bread—the Source of healing—added: "What and if ye shall see the Son of man ascend up where he was before? It is the spirit that quickeneth; the flesh profiteth nothing" (John 6:62–63). This is the reason why many find it hard to meet the Healer. They do not know the Holy Spirit. They do not know God spiritually.

The sun in the heavens might as well be a ball of ice were it not for the atmosphere that attracts its warmth and light to us and diffuses them through our world. And Christ's life and love only reach us through the Holy Spirit, the Light, the Atmosphere, the divine Medium who brings and sheds abroad His life and light, His love and presence in our being. He takes of the things of Christ and shows them to us, extracting His life and sweetly diffusing it through every part of our being. He is the great Quickener.

It was through the Holy Spirit that the Lord cast out devils on earth. And now, "if the Spirit of him that raised up Jesus from the dead dwell in you, he that raised up Christ from the dead shall also quicken your mortal [body] by his Spirit that dwelleth in you" (Romans 8:11).

Free Grace . . .

This new life must come, like all the blessings of Christ's redemption, as the free grace of God, without works and without distinction of merit or respect of persons.

Everything that comes through Christ must come as grace. There can be no works mingled with justifying faith. So our healing must be wholly of God, or not of grace at all. If Christ heals, He must do it alone. This principle ought to settle the question of using "means" in connection with faith for healing. The natural and the spiritual, the earthly and the heavenly, the works of man and the grace of God cannot be mixed any more than a person could expect to harness a tortoise with a locomotive. They cannot work together.

The gifts of the gospel are sovereign gifts. God can do the most difficult things for us Himself. But He does not help our self-sufficiency to do the easiest. A hopeless case is, therefore, much more hopeful than one where we think we can do something ourselves. We must venture on Him wholly.

If healing is to be sought by natural means, let

us obtain all the best results of skill and experience. But if it is to be received through the
name of Jesus, it must be by grace alone.

. . . *Freely Given*

It follows also in the same connection that if
healing is a part of the gospel and a gift of Christ,
it must be an impartial one, limited only by the
great "whosoever" of the gospel. It is not a special
gift of discriminating favoritism, but a great and
common heritage of faith and obedience. It is
"whosoever will, let him take the water of life
freely." It is true that all who come must conform
to the simple conditions of obedient faith. But
these are impartial, without respect of persons
and within the reach of all who trust and obey.

The simple condition of this great blessing—
the condition of all the blessings of the gospel—is
faith without sight. Grace without works and
faith without sight must always go together as
twin principles of the gospel. The one thing God
asks from all who are to receive His grace is that
they shall trust His simple Word. But this must
be real trust. We must believe and doubt not. If
God's Word be true at all, it is absolutely and utterly true.

With its living roots, a very small seed can split
open great rocks and mountains, but the germ
must be intact. One little laceration may kill its
life. One doubt will destroy the efficacy of faith;
therefore, it must begin by our taking God simply
at His Word. A faith that is going to wait for

signs and evidence will never be strong. Plants that begin by leaning will always need support. Indeed, the "faith" which rests upon seeing is not faith. "Blessed are they that have not seen, and yet have believed."

Abraham had to believe God and take the new name of faith and fatherhood before there was any indication of the answer. Indeed, every natural sign contradicted and stultified the promise. It is beautiful to notice the form of expression in Genesis 17. First Abraham was told, "Thou shalt be a father of many nations" (17:4). Then came the change of his name from Abram ("exalted father") to Abraham ("father of many"). It was the profession of his faith and the acknowledgment before a scorning world that he believed God.

Then follows God's next word. And how wonderful! The tense is changed. It is no longer a promise but an accomplished fact: "A father of many nations have I made thee" (17:5). Faith has turned the future into the past, and now God calls "things which are not" as though they were (see 1 Corinthians 1:28). So we must believe and receive the healing life of Jesus and all the blessings of the gospel.

More Than an Option

Are we under an obligation to seek divine healing of the body? Is it an optional matter with us how we shall be healed—whether we shall trust God or look to man?

Is this not "a statute and an ordinance" for us, too, and a matter of simple obedience? Is it not God's great prerogative to deal with the bodies He has redeemed, and an impertinence for us to choose some other way than His? Is not the gospel of salvation a commandment as well as a promise, and is not the gospel of healing of equal authority?

Has God not chosen to legislate about the way in which the plague of sin that has entered His world shall be dealt with? Have we any business to interfere with His great health promise? Has He not at enormous cost provided a remedy for the bodies of His children as part of His redemption, and is He not jealous for the honor and rights of His dear Son's name in this matter?

Does He not claim to be the Owner of His children's bodies, and does He not claim the right to care for them? Has He not left us one great prescription for disease, and is not any other course unauthorized and followed at our own risk? Surely these questions answer themselves. They leave but one course open to every child of God to whom He gives the light to see that His Word is "yea" and "Amen."

God's Fixed Principles

The order of God's dealings with our souls and bodies is regulated by certain fixed principles. The Bible was written to state them in plain language for the wayfaring man. God works from within outward, beginning with our spiritual nature and then diffusing His life and power through our physical being.

Many persons come to God for healing whose spiritual life is wholly defective and wrong. God does not always refuse the healing. He begins in the depths of the soul, and when the soul is prepared to receive His life, He may begin to heal the body.

There is a close relation between the state of the soul and the body. John prays that Gaius "mayest prosper and be in health, even as thy soul prospereth" (3 John 2). A little cloud of sin upon the heart will leave a shadow upon the brain and nerves and a pressure upon the whole frame. A malicious breath of spiritual evil will poison the blood and depress the whole system. But a clear, calm and confident spirit will bring vigor into all the physical life. It will open the way for all the full pulses of the Lord's life in us.

Hence, also, healing will often be gradual in its development as the spiritual life grows and faith takes a firmer hold of Christ. The principle of the divine life, like the natural, is "first the blade, then the ear, after that the full corn in the ear." Many people want the head of wheat while the blade is yet tender. But it would only overwhelm us by its weight. We must have deep and quiet strength to sustain our higher blessing.

Sometimes this preparation is completed beforehand. Then God can work very rapidly. But in each case He knows the order and process best adapted to the development of the whole

man. That is ever His great end in all His work-
ings in us.

Some Limitations

Any limitations there may be of healing are also
fixed by certain principles. Some enter not into
this promised land because of unbelief and because they are a stiff-necked generation. Sometimes someone asks, "Why should people ever die
if Christ will always heal?" Because faith can only
go as far as God's promise, and God has nowhere
promised that we shall never die during this dispensation. It is not immortal life that God
promises in connection with the healing of the
mortal body. The promise is fullness of life and
health and strength up to the measure of our
natural life and until our life work is done. True,
it is the life of the resurrection that we have; but
it is not the whole of it—only the firstfruits.

In speaking of our immortal life the apostle
says: "Now he that hath wrought us for the
selfsame thing is God, who also hath given unto
us the earnest of the Spirit" (2 Corinthians 5:5).
That is, as our earnest was a handful of the very
soil of the purchased farm, but only a handful, so
God has given us now by His Spirit in our new
physical life a handful of the very life of the resurrection. But it is only a handful, and the fullness
will not come until His coming. But that handful
is worth more than all the soil of earth.

Shall we have strength for all kinds of supernatural exploits and extraordinary exertions? We

have the promise of sufficient strength for all the will of God and all the service of Christ. But we shall have no strength for mere display and certainly none to waste in recklessness or spend in selfishness and sin.

Within the limits of our God-appointed work—and these limits may be very wide, much wider than any mere natural strength—we "can do all things through Christ which strengtheneth [us]." We may fearlessly undertake all labors, self-denials and difficulties in the face of exposure, weakness, conditions of climate and the most engrossing demands upon strength and time, where Christ clearly leads and calls us. We shall have His protecting power and find that "God is able to make all grace abound toward [us]; that [we], always having all sufficiency in all things, may abound to every good work" (2 Corinthians 9:8).

But let us touch the forbidden fruit, wander out of the sacred circle of His will or spend our strength on self or sin, and our life will lose its strength like Samson's arm and wither like Jonah's gourd. Yes, it must be true, always true, in our life as Paul says in Romans 11:36: "Of him, and through him, and to him, are all things: to whom be glory for ever. Amen."

CHAPTER 3

Popular Objections

There are currently a number of objections to the glad tidings that He who "forgiveth all [our] iniquities" as truly and as fully also "healeth all [our] diseases." I shall refer to some of the more forcible.

Objection 1: *The age of miracles is past.* This is commonly assumed as an axiom and almost quoted as a Bible text.

In reply let me ask: What age are we in? There have been, and shall be, various ages and dispensations. There was the Edenic, the Patriarchal, the Mosaic. There will be the Millennial, the Eternal. We are presently in the Christian era.

But perhaps there is more than one Christian age: one for Christ and His apostles and one for us. Yet Paul says he lived in "these last days." He speaks of the people of his generation as those on whom "the ends of the world are come." And

Peter, in his sermon on the day of Pentecost, claims for his day a prophecy of Joel for the latter days.

We must then be in the age of Christ and Christianity. And if this is not the age of miracles, then what is it?

But perhaps there was to be a great gulf between the first and last periods of this age. Perhaps it was only to begin with special manifestations of divine power and then shade down into sober commonplace. Why then should Joel say that the signal outpouring of the Holy Spirit should be "in the last days"? Why should he say that the supernatural signs and wonders both in earth and heaven should be especially "before the great and the terrible day of the LORD come" (Joel 2:31)—that is, toward the close of the Christian age and prior to Jesus' second advent?

Why also should Paul so strongly insist that Christ's Church is one body, not two, and that the gifts of every part belong to the whole (see 1 Corinthians 12)? If there is an essential difference between the apostolic and a later age, then the church is not one body but two; then the gifts of those members do not flow into our members; then the glorious figure and powerful reasoning of that chapter are false and delusive. If we are the same body, we have the same life and power.

Were the Apostles Different?

What made the apostles more mighty than ordinary men? It was not their companionship with Jesus; it was the gift of the Holy Spirit. Have we not the same? And do we not exalt the men and disparage the Spirit that made them what they were when we speak of their power as exceptional and transient?

Peculiar and exceptional functions they indeed had as witnesses of Christ's resurrection and the organizers of the church on earth. But to show to men that the miraculous gifts of the church were not confined to them, these gifts are specially distinguished from the apostleship in First Corinthians 12. They were conferred in preeminent degree on Stephen, Philip and others who were not apostles at all, and they were committed by James to the ordinary and permanent eldership of the church. No, our dear Master never contemplated or proposed any post-apostolic gulf of impotence and failure.

Mankind's unbelief and sin have made such a gulf. The church's own corruption has caused it. But Christ never desired it. See Him standing on the Galilean mountain midway between earth and heaven. See Him looking down to our century with a love as tender, a grace as full and a power as available as He exercised in the first. Hear Him speaking in the present tense, as though we were all equally near to Him who would never be separated from us: "All power is given unto me in heaven and in earth. . . . Lo, I am with you all the days, even unto the end of the age" (Matthew 28:18–20, Greek).

Just One Age

It was to be one age, not two, and Christ's "all power" has never been withdrawn. He was to be a perpetual I Am, to be as near at the end as at the beginning. The work we are to do is to be the complement of His own. In fact, it *is* His own work, for Luke says He "began both to do and teach" (Acts 1:1). He must, therefore, be continuing His work still.

This is just what Jesus said our work would be: "He that believeth on me, the works that I do shall he do also" (John 14:12)—that is, these works shall be Christ's and ours, in partnership. Neither shall they be in any way diminished by His seeming absence, for "greater works . . . shall he do; because I go unto my Father."

Indeed, as long as the ancient church retained in even limited measure the faith and holiness of the first days, the same works were uniformly found. In the second, third and fourth centuries, fathers as famous as Irenaeus and Tertullian bore testimony to the prevalence of many undoubted miracles of healing and even the raising of the dead in the name of Jesus. And as late as the fifth century supernatural events were attested by authorities as high as Procopius and Justinian on evidence so strong that the sober editor Mosheim declared that he who would doubt it must be ready to question all the facts of history.

We Are in the Age of Miracles

The age of miracles is not past. The Word of God never indicated a hint of such a fact. On the contrary, miracles are to be among the signs of the last days. The very adversary himself is to counterfeit them and send forth unto the kings of the earth demon spirits working miracles. The only defense against the false miracles will be the true.

We are in the age of miracles, the age of Christ, the age that lies between the two advents. Underneath the eye of a ceaseless divine Presence, this is the age of power, the age which above all other ages of time should be intensely alive.

Objection 2. *The same results as are claimed for faith in the healing of disease are also said to follow the practices of spiritism, animism, clairvoyance and the like.* Although some of the manifestations of spiritism are undoubted frauds, we will not deny that many are unquestionably supernatural, produced by forces for which physical science has no explanation.

It is no use to try to meet this monster of spiritism with the hasty and shallow denial of the facts. It is no use to try to explain spiritism as trickery. These manifestations often are real and superhuman. They are "the spirits of devils, working miracles" (Revelation 16:14). They are the revived forces of the Egyptian magicians, the Grecian oracles, the Roman haruspices, the Indian fakirs. They are not divine. They are less than omnipotent, but they are more than human.

Our Lord has expressly warned us of them and told us to test them, not by their power but by their fruits—their holiness, humility and homage to the name of Jesus and the Word of God. Their very existence renders it imperative that we should be able to present against them—like the rod of Moses that swallowed the magicians' rods and at last silenced their limited power—the living forces of a holy Christianity in the physical as well as the spiritual world.

Objection 3. *The miracles of Christ and His apostles were designed to establish the facts and doctrines of Christianity; we do not need their continuance.* But the critics continue to call in question the existence of these facts and the credibility of these writings. And how are the inhabitants of new countries to know the divine origin of these oracles? What access have they, or indeed the great masses of men everywhere, to the archives of learning or the manuscripts of the Bible?

We Need to See a Living Christ

No, every generation needs a living Christ, and every new community needs these "signs following" to confirm the Word. And we have sometimes seen the plausible and persistent agnostic, whom no reason could satisfy, silenced and confounded when brought face to face with some humble, unlettered woman as she told him with glowing, convincing honesty that she had been raised up from lifelong helplessness by the Word and name of Jesus only.

Until Christ returns, the world will never cease to need the touch of His power and presence. "God also bearing them witness, both with signs and wonders . . . and gifts of the Holy Ghost, according to his own will" (Hebrews 2:4).

There is also a current misapprehension about the full design of Christ's miracles that takes away half their beauty and value. They are looked upon mainly, even solely, as special testimonies to Christ's power and deity. But if this had been all, a few special and marked cases would have been sufficient. He would not then have healed the thousands who daily thronged Him. But we are told, on the contrary, that they were not isolated and occasional but numerous and almost universal.

Jesus Had to Be True to His Character

Christ healed all who had need of healing and all who were sick. This was not only a proof of His power, but a demonstration of what He now wished them to know—His boundless love. Jesus healed to fulfill the ancient prophetic picture of the Messiah: "Himself took our infirmities, and bare our sicknesses." But if it was necessary then for Him to fulfill that character, it is as much so now. He must never cease to be true to the picture God drew of Him and which He also drew of Himself.

If this is not true still for us, then Jesus Christ is not "the same yesterday, and to day, and for ever." If this is not still true for us, then—perhaps—the other promises of the Scriptures are also not true for us, and He has not borne our sins any more than our sickness and suffering. No, His heart is still the same.

Objection 4. *Christ's last promise in Mark embraces much more than healing; if you claim one, you must claim all.* If you expect the healing of the sick, you must also include the gift of tongues and the power to overcome malignant poisons. We cheerfully accept this severe logic. We cannot afford to give up one of the promises.

We admit our belief in the presence of the Healer in all the *charismata* of the early church. We see no reason why a humble servant of Christ, engaged in the Master's work, may not claim in simple faith the power to resist malaria and other poisons and malignant dangers. To a greater or less extent the gift of tongues has been continuous in the church of Christ and, along with many counterfeits, has undoubtedly been realized in the present generation.

Objection 5. *Glory accrues to God from our submission to His will in sickness; the results of sanctified affliction are blessed.* Perhaps no objection is more strongly urged. And if those who urge and claim to practice this suggestion would really accept their sickness and lie passive under it, they would at least be consistent. But do they not send for a doctor and do their best to get out of this "sweet will of God"? Is this meekly submitting to the affliction? Does not the submission usually come when the result is known to be inevitable?

Christian Discipline Is Misunderstood

We do not deny the happy results of many a case of painful sickness in turning the soul from some forbidden path and leading it into deeper experiences. Nor do we question the fervent piety of many an invalid who cannot trust God for healing. But we are sure there is an immense amount of vague and unscriptural misunderstanding with respect to the principles of Christian discipline.

The Word says, "For this cause many are weak and sickly among you, and many sleep. For if we would judge ourselves, we should not be judged" (1 Corinthians 11:30–31). Here is a definite and unchangeable law of God's dealings with His dear children. When we are judging ourselves, we shall not be judged. While we hearken and obey, He "will put none of these diseases" upon us that He "brought upon the Egyptians" (Exodus 15:26). The normal state for God's faithful children is soundness of spirit and soul and body (see 1 Thessalonians 5:23).

God's desire for His children is that they may "prosper be in health, even as [their] soul[s] prospereth" (3 John 2). His will for them is to act in these things according to His Word. He wants for them "the good pleasure of his goodness" (2 Thessalonians 1:11) and "that good, and acceptable, and perfect, will of God" (Romans 12:2). "Many," it is true, "are the afflictions of the righteous." But it is also true that "the LORD delivereth him out of them all. He keepeth all his bones: not one of them is broken" (Psalm 34:19–20).

Affliction and Sickness Are Not the Same

Between "affliction" and "sickness" there is a very clear distinction. At Marah the children of Israel drank bitter water that God purified (Exodus 15:23ff.), just as many a trial is sanctified and blessed. It was *there* that He made a statute and an ordinance of healing. He told the people that if they would obey Him they should not be sick, for He would be their constant Healer. In exact parallel, James says to us (5:13): "Is any . . . afflicted? let him pray"—that is, for grace and strength. But (5:14), "Is any sick among you? let him call for the elders of the church" to pray for healing.

Affliction is suffering with Christ, and He was not sick. Jesus warned, "In the world ye shall have tribulation" (John 16:33). All the more we need a sound, strong heart to bear and overcome.

Objection 6. *We are presumptuous to claim the healing of disease absolutely*. Rather, the model of all true prayer is Christ's language in the Garden: "Not as I will, but as thou wilt" (Matthew 26:39). Bowing to the divine will is the believer's best course, but these objectors have forgotten that Jesus also said on that occasion in Gethsemane, "Save me from this hour: but for this cause came I unto this hour. Father, glorify thy name" (John 12:27–28).

Indeed, there are many who believe that our Lord's prayer in Gethsemane was answered by the Father, saving Him from Satan's attempt to take His life prematurely in the Garden. In Hebrews we are told He "was heard in that he feared" (5:7). Certainly, in any such circumstances, when prompted by extreme distress to ask for something for which we have no clear warrant, promise or favorable intimation of the divine will, we ought ever to refer the matter to the arbitration of that unknown will.

God Has Made Known His Will

But when we know from God's own Word to us that a blessing is in accordance with His will, that it is provided for, purchased and promised, is it not really evasive to come to Him in doubt and uncertainty? Is it not very much the same as if a son at college should continue to write, asking his father's permission for things for which he had already been given the fullest directions in his father's first letter?

Did Christ thus pray when he asked for things He knew to be consistent with God's will? At Bethany, prior to raising Lazarus, He said, "Father, I thank thee that thou hast heard me" (John 11:41). Is it not as lawful for us to imitate

Him in His prayer at Bethany as in His prayer at Gethsemane?

When God's will is clearly made known, may we not pray even as Christ prayed? Jesus told His disciples, "If ye abide in me, and my words abide in you, ye shall ask what ye will, and it shall be done unto you" (John 15:7). Do we pray in indefiniteness when we ask forgiveness? We take it, we claim it, and being strong in faith we thus glorify God.

Objection 7. *There are many cases of failure; look at Paul and his companions who were ill.* Paul's thorn is inevitably kept as a precious relic to torment doubting Christians, and Trophimus and Epaphroditus are dragged forward on their couches to encourage the willing patient in the Hospital of Doubting Castle.

With regard to Paul's thorn we must say four things:

> *(1) It is not at all certain that it was disease. It was a messenger of Satan to buffet him— some humiliation, perhaps stammering.*
>
> *(2) It was so far healed and more than healed, whatever it was, that it brought the power of Christ to rest upon Paul so mightily that he was abundantly enabled for all his labors and duties. He longed for more such provocations of blessing. And he who can see in this a feeble invalid laid aside from work is afflicted with spiritual cross-eyes!*

(3) Before people can claim that their sickness is a heavenly visitation like Paul's to keep them from being exalted above measure, they would need to have been up in the third heaven with him and to hear things unlawful for a person to utter!

(4) Paul does give us elsewhere the account of his healing (see 2 Corinthians 1:8–11). It was unmistakably by believing prayer and mighty faith in "God that raiseth the dead."

As for Epaphroditus, he was healed through God's mercy. Trophimus may also have been healed, although his healing was delayed.

Healing Is Not Always Instantaneous

Healing, even by faith, is not always instantaneous. There are "miracles" and "gifts of healing," the one sudden and stupendous, the other simple and probably gradual. That Trophimus should have been to blame for his illness or slowness of faith is not remarkable. But that there should be only two such cases in all these inspired personal sketches is most remarkable!

There are still instances of failure, but perhaps they may be accounted for through defective knowledge or unbelief, or through disobedience to God in some way. There may be failure to follow consistently the teachings of the Word and the Spirit, or the sickness may be for a deeper spiritual discipline. And there are failures in the spiritual life from the same or similar causes.

These failures in no way disprove the reality of the divine promises or the sufficiency of Christ's grace. "Let God be true" even if "every man a liar" (Romans 3:4).

Objection 8. *If these things are so, people should never die*. Why not? Why should faith go further than the Word? Anything beyond that is presumption.

The Word places a limit to human life, and all that scriptural faith can claim is sufficiency of health and strength for our life work and within its fair limits. It may be longer or shorter, but we need not, like the wicked, live out less than half our days (see Psalm 55:23). Our life should be complete, satisfying and long enough for the work God has given us to do. And then, when the close comes, why need it be with painful and depressing sickness, as the rotten apple falls in June from disease and with a worm at its core?

Why may it not rather be as that ripe apple would drop in September—mature, mellow and ready to fall without a struggle into the gardener's hand? So Job pictures the close of a good man's life "in a full age, like as a shock of corn cometh in in his season" (Job 5:26).

Objection 9. *Did not God make all these "means," and does He not want us to use them?* Indeed, is it not presumption for us to expect God to do anything unless we first do all we can for ourselves? In reply I answer, God has nowhere prescribed medical "means," and we have no right to infer that drugs are ordinarily His "means." They are not again and again referred to, like food, as necessary or enjoined for our use.

The Bible Mentions Few Doctors

It is a singular, unanswerable fact that in the whole history of the patriarchs no reference is made to the use of medicines. In the story of Job, so full of vivid details, everyone else is described but the doctor, and everything in the universe but medications. There is no physician in attendance or surely we should have caught a glimpse of him. When Job recovers, it is wholly from God's direct hand after Job finds his true place of humility to God and love to man.

In the still more elaborate prescriptions and prohibitions of Leviticus, even including procedures for dealing with the disease of leprosy, there is not even a remote intimation of a doctor or a drugstore. It is not until after the time of Solomon and the importation, no doubt, of Egypt's godless culture and science that we find the first definite case of medical treatment. There King Asa, the patient, dies—and dies under the stigma of unbelief and declension from God.

In the New Testament, medical practice is referred to in terms not at all complimentary when the woman who touched the hem of Jesus' garment is described. Luke abandoned his practice as a physician for evangelistic work. While he was present with Paul in Melita at the healing of the father of Publius, it was Paul who "laid his hands on him [Publius], and healed him" (Acts 28:8). Surely this was so the Lord Jesus should have all the glory. Moreover, it was so His saints in these latter days should have the comfort of knowing that the healing was done in the presence of a physician whose medical skills were never used—as far as the record goes—after his conversion.

Without going further, this much at least is clear: (1) God has not prescribed medicine. (2) God has prescribed another way of healing in the name of Jesus, has provided for it in the atonement, has appointed an ordinance for its application, has commanded and enjoined it.

All the provisions of grace are by faith, not by works or "means." The use of remedies, if successful, usually gives the glory to man, and God will not permit that. If the healing of sickness is one of the purchases of Christ's atonement and one of His prerogatives as our Redeemer, then He is jealous for it, and we should also be jealous.

Recognize the "Law of Faith"

If healing is part of the plan of salvation, then we know that the whole plan is framed according to the "law of faith." If the language of James is a command, then it excludes the treatment of disease by human remedies as much as the employment of one physician would exclude the treatment of another at the same time and for the same case.

If that is God's way of healing, then other methods must be man's ways, and there must be some risk in deliberately repudiating the former for the latter. We do not imply by this that the medical profession is sinful or the use of means always wrong. There may be—there always will be—instances where faith cannot be exercised. And if natural means have—as they do have—a limited value, there is ample room for their employment in these cases. But for the trusting and obedient child of God, there is the more excellent way that His Word has clearly prescribed. By it, God's name will be ever glorified afresh and our spiritual life continually renewed.

Our age is one of increasing rationalism. Unbelief is constantly endeavoring to eliminate all traces of direct supernatural working from the universe and to explain everything by second causes and natural development. For this very reason, God wants to show His immediate working wherever our faith will afford Him an opportunity. Higher criticism is industriously taking the miraculous from our Bibles, and a lower standard of Christian life is busy taking all that is divine out of our lives.

Let all who believe in a living God be willing to prove to a scoffing generation that "the everlasting God, the LORD, the Creator of the ends of the earth, fainteth not, neither is weary" (Isaiah 40:28). Let them proclaim that "in him we live, and move, and have our being" (Acts 17:28) and that still there is nothing too hard for the Lord.

Objection 10. *Divine healing unduly exalts the physical body and directs the minds of people from the transcendent interest of the immortal soul, promoting fanaticism and leading to other evils.* The same objection might be brought against the years of our Lord's ministry on earth, when the healing of the body was made an avenue to reach men's souls and a testimony of His spiritual teachings. The doctrine of Christ's healing power is closely linked with the necessity of holiness and the deeper truths and experiences of the spiritual life. It tends, in a preeminent degree, to promote purity and earnestness.

The power that heals the body usually imparts a much richer baptism of the Holy Spirit to the heart. The retaining of this divine life and health requires constant fellowship with God and prompts consecrated service for the Master. The spiritual results far outweigh the temporal.

Divine healing is one of the most powerful checks and impulses in the lives of those who have truly received it. The abuses complained of will usually be found connected with false teaching and unscriptural perversions that rash or ambitious persons disseminate for their own ungodly ends.

A Humbling, Holy Truth

The true doctrine of healing through the Lord Jesus Christ is most humbling, holy and practical.

It exalts no man; it spares no sin; it offers no promises to the disobedient; it gives no strength for selfish indulgence or worldly ends. Rather, it exalts the name of Jesus, glorifies God, inspires the soul with faith and power, summons to a life of self-denial and holy service. It awakens a slumbering church and an unbelieving world with the solemn signals of a living God and a risen Christ.

Extravagances, perversions and counterfeits we know there are. Unauthorized and self-constituted healers and mercenary impostors abound. There are rash and indiscriminate anointings of persons that discredit the truth. But the truth of God is not chargeable with human error, and the counterfeit is often a startling testimony to the existence of the genuine.

Let the ministers of the Lord Jesus answer these evils by claiming and exercising, in the power of the Holy Spirit, the gifts and offices once delivered to them. In the words found in Malachi 3:18, let the people of God in these perilous times "discern between the righteous and the wicked, between him that serveth God and him that serveth him not."

CHAPTER
4

Practical Directions

Together we have considered the scriptural grounds of the doctrine of healing by faith in God. The practical question arises next: How can a person who fully believes in the doctrine receive the blessing and appropriate healing?

I suggest seven steps.

Be Fully Persuaded

First, *be fully persuaded of the Word of God in this matter of divine healing.* The Word is the only sure foundation of rational and scriptural faith. Your faith must rest on the great principles and promises of the Bible or it can never stand the testings that are sure to come. You must be so sure that this is part of the gospel and the redemption of Christ that all the reasonings of the best of men and women cannot shake you.

Most of the practical failures of faith in this matter result from defective or doubtful convictions concerning the divine Word. A woman who had fully embraced this truth and accepted Christ as her Healer was immediately strengthened very much both in spirit and body. Her overflowing heart was only too glad to tell the good news to all her friends. Among others, she met her pastor and told him of her faith and blessing.

To her surprise, he immediately objected to any such views. He warned her against this new fanaticism and told her that these promises on which she was resting were not for us but only for the apostles and the apostolic age. She listened, questioned, yielded and abandoned her confidence. In less than one month, when I saw her again, she had sunk to such depression that she scarcely knew whether she even believed the Bible.

If those promises were for the apostles, she argued, why might not all the other promises of the Bible also be for them only? I invited her to spend time examining the teaching of the Word of God. We carefully compared the promises of healing from Exodus to James. Every question we calmly weighed until the truth became so manifest and its evidence so overwhelming that she could only say, "I know it is here, and I know it is true, even if all the world should deny it!"

Then she knelt and asked the Lord's forgiveness for her weakness and unbelief. She renewed her solemn profession of faith and consecration and claimed again the promise of healing and the baptism of the Holy Spirit. From that day she has

been restored and blessed with all spiritual blessings. The very pastor who caused her to stumble
has been forced to own that this is the finger of
God. But the starting point of all her blessing was
the moment when she fully accepted and rested
in the living Word.

God countenances not the slightest departure
from His Word. When God said to Moses,
"Speak ye unto the rock," Moses used "means"
and with his rod "smote the rock twice" (Numbers 20:8,11). God declared, "Because ye believed
me not, to sanctify me in the eyes of the children
of Israel, therefore ye shall not bring this congregation into the land which I have given them"
(20:12).

Moses suffered severely for his departure from
instructions, but God in His own way was
sanctified.

Be Assured of God's Will

Second, *be fully assured of the will of God to heal
you.* Most persons are ready enough to admit the
power of Christ to heal. The devil himself admits
this. True faith implies equal confidence in the
willingness of God to answer the prayer of faith.
Any doubt on this point will surely paralyze your
prayer for definite healing. If there is any question of God's will to heal *you*, there can be no certainty in your expectation.

A mere vague trust in the possible acceptance of
your prayer is not faith definite enough to grap-
ple with the forces of disease and death. The

prayer for healing, "if it be Thy will," carries with it no claim for which Satan will quit his hold. This is a matter about which you ought to know His will before you ask, and then you must will and claim it because it is His will.

Has God given you any means by which you may know His will? Most assuredly. If the Lord Jesus has purchased healing for you in His redemption, it must be God's will for you to have it, for Christ's whole redeeming work was simply the executing of the Father's will. If Jesus has promised it to you, it must be His will that you should receive it, for how can you know His will but by His Word?

More than that, if the Lord Jesus has bequeathed healing to you in the New Testament, which is simply His last will and testament, then it is one of the bequests of your Savior's will, secured to all the blood-bought heirs of God and joint-heirs with Christ. If you are to partake of any of the benefits, you must observe all the terms of His testament. Therefore, all questions of your wishes or desires in the matter must end when the will of God is defined and proved.

The Word of God is forever the standard of His will, and that Word has declared immutably that it is God's greatest desire and unalterable principle of action to give to every person according as he or she will believe. Especially has He promised to save all who will receive Christ by faith and to heal all who will receive healing by similar faith. No one thinks of asking for forgiveness "if it be Thy will." Nor should you throw any stronger doubt on His promise of physical redemption. Both are freely offered to every trusting person who will accept them.

Some of us prayed with and anointed for healing a woman quite prominent in Christian work. She returned in a few weeks saying that she was no better. Asked if she had believed fully, she replied, "I believed that I should be healed if it was His good pleasure, and if not, I am willing to have it otherwise."

"But," I responded, "may we not know God's pleasure in this matter from His own Word and ask with the full expectation of the blessing? Indeed, ought we to ask anything of God until we have reason to believe that it is His will? Is not His Word the intimation of His will; and, after He has so fully promised it, is it not a vexation and a mockery to imply a doubt of His willingness?"

She went away, and the very next morning she claimed the promise. She told the Lord that now she not only believed that He could, but would and did remove the trouble. In less than half an hour an external tumor of considerable size had wholly, visibly disappeared.

Often there is much subtle unbelief in the prayer, "Thy will be done." That blessed petition really expresses the highest measure of divine love and blessing. No kinder thing can come to us than that will. And yet we often ask it as if it was the iron hand of a cruel despot and an inexorable destiny. This leads us to say with Job: "Though he slay me, yet will I trust in him."

One doctor who really believed the Bible to be the inspired Word of God actually put his belief to the test by first saying to every patient at the first interview, "Are you a Christian?" If the patient answered affirmatively, his reply was, "I cannot prescribe any medicine for you because it is not medical healing that will cure you. Are you willing to put your case in the hands of the Lord Jesus Christ?" If the answer was still yes, he would pray and explain to the patient how he or she could have healing from the Lord. He would treat with medicine only those who said they were not Christians.

It should be added that that doctor was the most successful medical practitioner for miles around. He always had more patients than he could deal with personally.

Are You Right with God?

Third, *be careful that you are right with God.* If your sickness has come to you on account of any sinful cause, be sure that you thoroughly repent of and confess your sins and make all restitution as far as it is in your power. If sickness has been a discipline designed to separate you from some evil, at once present yourself to God in frank self-judgment and consecration and claim from Him the grace to sanctify you and keep you holy.

An impure heart is a constant fountain of disease. A sanctified spirit is in itself as wholesome as it is holy. At the same time, do not let Satan paralyze your faith by throwing you back on your unworthiness, telling you that you are not good enough to claim healing. You never can deserve any of God's mercies. The only plea is the name, the merits and the righteousness of Christ. But you can renounce known sin and you can walk so as to please God.

You can judge yourself and put away all that God shows you to be wrong. The moment you do this you are forgiven. "If we would judge ourselves, we should not be judged" (1 Corinthians 11:31). "If we confess our sins, he is faithful and just to forgive us our sins, and to cleanse us from all unrighteousness" (1 John 1:9). Do not wait to feel forgiveness or joy, but let your will be wholly turned to God, and believe at once that you are accepted. Then "draw near with a true heart in full assurance of faith, having [your heart] sprinkled from an evil conscience, and [your body] washed with pure water" (Hebrews 10:22).

It is quite vain for you to try to exercise faith for yourself or others in the face of willful transgression and in defiance of the chastening that God has meant you should respect and yield to. But when you receive His correction and turn to Him with humble and obedient heart, He may then graciously remove the pain and make the touch of healing the token of His forgiving love. "The prayer of faith shall save the sick, and the Lord shall raise him up; and if he have committed sins, they shall be forgiven him. Confess your faults one to another, and pray one for another, that ye may be healed" (James 5:15–16).

Often sickness is a moral malaria contracted by infringing on Satan's territory. You cannot be healed until you step away from the forbidden place and stand again on holy ground. Thus this question of your personal state, while not a condition of healing, is a very important element in it.

The great purpose of God in all His dealings with us is our highest welfare and our spiritual soundness. To the suffering Christian, therefore, there is no better counsel than the old exhortation: "The LORD is good unto them that wait for him. . . . He doth not afflict willingly nor grieve the children of men. . . . Let us search and try our ways, and turn again to the LORD" (Lamentations 3:25, 33, 40).

Commit and Claim

Fourth, having become fully persuaded of the Word of God, the will of God and your own personal acceptance with God, now *commit your body to God and claim by simple faith His promise of healing in the name of Jesus.* Do not merely ask for it, but humbly and firmly claim healing as His covenant pledge, as your inheritance, as a purchased redemption right. Claim it as something already fully offered you in the gospel and waiting only your acceptance to make good your possession.

There is a great difference between asking and taking, between expecting and accepting. You must take Christ as your Healer—not as an experiment, not as a future benefit, but as a present reality. You must believe that He does now, according to His promise, touch your life with His almighty hand and quicken the fountains of your being with His strength. Do not merely believe that He will do so, but claim and believe that He does now touch you and begins the work of healing in your body. And go forth counting it done, acknowledging and praising Him for it.

It is a good thing to prepare for this solemn act of committal and appropriating faith. It ought to be a very deliberate and final step. In the nature of things it cannot be repeated. Like the marriage ceremony, it is the signalizing and sealing of a great transaction. It depends for its value upon the reality of the union that it seals.

Before you take this step you should weigh each question thoroughly and then regard it as forever settled. You should step out solemnly, definitely, irrevocably on new ground, on God's promise, with the deep conviction that it is forever. This gives great strength and rest to the heart. It closes the door against a thousand doubts and temptations.

From that moment, doubt should be regarded as absolutely out of the question and even the thought of retreating to old "means" inadmissible. God has become the Physician, and He will not give His glory to another. God has healed, and all human attempts at helping would imply a doubt of the reality of the healing.

When God makes it plain that death is approaching, it would not appear to be unscriptural to call in a doctor, as the state officer lawfully appointed by the powers that be, to whom we are instructed to be obedient.

The more entirely the act of faith can be a complete committal, the more power will it have. If you have any question about your faith for this, make it a matter of special preparation and prayer. Ask God to give you special faith for this act. All your graces must come from Him, and faith is among them. You have nothing of your own, and even your very faith is but the grace of Christ Himself within you. You can exercise faith, and thus far your responsibility extends. But God must impart faith, and you simply put it on and wear it as from Him. This makes the exercise of strong faith a very simple and blessed possibility.

Jesus does not say to you, "Have great faith yourself." But He does say, "Have the faith of God." God's faith is all-sufficient, and you can have it and use it. You can take Christ for your faith as you took Him for your justification, for your victories over temptation, for your sanctification. You may then rest in the assurance that your faith has not failed to meet the demands of the promise, for it has been Christ's own faith.

You simply come in His name and present Him as your perfect offering, your plea, your faith, your advocate, your righteousness. Your very faith itself is nothing but simply taking His free gift of grace. Come and claim His promise. And, having done so, believe according to His Word that you have received it.

Act Your Faith

Fifth, *act your faith*. To the paralyzed man, Jesus commanded, "Arise, and take up thy bed, and go thy way" (Mark 2:11). Not to show your faith or display your courage, but *because of* your faith begin to act as one who is healed. Treat Christ as if you trusted Him by attempting in His Name and strength what would be impossible in your own. He will not fail you if you really trust Him and continue to act your faith consistently and courageously. But it is most important that you not do this on human faith or word.

Do not rise from your bed or walk on your lame foot because somebody tells you to do so. That is not faith but impression. God will surely tell you to do so, but it must be at His Word. If you are walking with Him and trusting Him, you will know His voice. Your prayer, like Peter's, must be, "Lord, . . . bid me come unto thee on the water," and He will surely bid you if He is to heal you. But in this great and solemn work, you must know and see the Lord for yourself.

Remember the Lord's words to Peter when he began to sink: "O thou of little faith, wherefore didst thou doubt?" (Matthew 14:31). When you do go forth to act your faith, be careful not to begin to watch the result or look at the symptoms or see if you stand.

You must ignore all symptoms and see only God there before you, almighty to sustain you and save you from falling. The gardener who digs up his seed to see if it is growing will very soon kill his plants at the root. The true farmer trusts nature and lets the seed grow in silence. So trust God, willing even to see the answer buried like that seed and dying in the dark soil of discouragement. You can know that "if it die, it bringeth forth much fruit" (John 12:24).

Be Prepared for Trials

Sixth, *be prepared for trials of faith*. Do not look necessarily for the immediate removal of the symptoms. Do not think of them. Simply ignore them and press forward, claiming the reality back of all symptoms. Remember the health you have claimed is not your own natural strength, but the life of Jesus manifested in your mortal flesh. Therefore, the old natural life may still be encompassed with many infirmities, but back of it and over against it is the all-sufficient life of Christ to sustain your body. "Ye are dead, and your life is hid with Christ in God" (Colossians 3:3). But Christ is your life (3:4), and "the life [you] now live in the flesh [you] live by the faith of the Son of God, who loved [you], and gave himself for [you]" (Galatians 2:20). Do not, then, wonder if nature fails you. The Lord's healing is not nature. It is grace. It is by the power of the risen Lord.

It is Christ who is your life. Christ's body is for

your body as His Spirit was for your spirit. Therefore, do not wonder if there should be trials. They come to show you your need of Christ and to throw you back upon Him. To know this and so to put on His strength in your weakness and live in it moment by moment is the way of perfect healing. Then, again, trials always test and strengthen faith in proportion as it is real. Faith must be shown to be genuine so that God can vindicate His reward of it before the whole universe.

It is thus that God increases your faith by laying larger demands upon it and compelling you to claim and exercise more grace. "As an eagle stirreth up her nest" and tumbles out her young in midair to compel them to reach out their little pinions, so God may push you off all your own props and confidences to compel you to reach out your wings of faith. But for the sacrifice of Isaac, Abraham might never have attained, as he did, to the faith of the resurrection.

Whatever the symptoms, you must steadily believe that back of them all, God is working out His own great restoration. "For which cause we faint not; but though our outward man perish, yet the inward man is renewed day by day" (2 Corinthians 4:16).

Use Your New Health for God

Seventh, *use your new strength and health for God, and be careful to obey the will of the Master.* This Christ-given strength is a very sacred thing. It is the resurrection life of Christ in you. And it must be spent as He Himself would spend it. It cannot be wasted on sin and selfishness. It must be given to God as "a living sacrifice" (Romans 12:1). The strength will fail when it is devoted to the world, and sin will always bring bodily chastisement. You may expect to "prosper and be in health, even as [your] soul prospereth."

Nor is it enough for you to use this healing for yourself. You must testify of it to others. You must tell it to the world. You must be a fearless and faithful witness to the gospel of full redemption. This is not a faith that you can hold to yourself. It is a great and solemn trust. In receiving it you must unite with others to use it for the glory of God, for a witness to the truth and for the spread of the gospel.

These wonderful manifestations of the power of God that we are beginning to see are perhaps significant signals of the end—forerunners of Christ's great appearing. As they marked the period of His presence on earth, so they will attend His return. And they bid us prepare solemnly and earnestly for His advent. Our eyes must no longer be on the grave but on the opening heavens. Our hearts must feel already some of the pulses of that resurrection life. It is ours to watch and work as none others can. We must not hold ourselves back in anxious self-care, but work in His great might, in season and out of season. And we shall find it true even as Christ said, "Whosoever will lose his life for my sake shall find it" (Matthew 16:25)—shall find it unto life eternal.

Thus let us claim and keep and consecrate this great gift of the gospel and the grace of God. In the words of Paul in First Thessalonians 5:23–24: "The very God of peace sanctify you wholly; and I pray God your whole spirit and soul and body be preserved blameless unto the coming of our Lord Jesus Christ. Faithful is he that calleth you, who also will do it."

CHAPTER 5

Testimonies from Scripture

The value of Scripture testimonies to the subject of divine healing cannot be questioned. They bring the gospel message down to the personal level and into contact with the sufferer as mere abstract teaching cannot do. Shall we glance at some of them?

The Patriarch Job

Job's physical affliction is the earliest fully detailed in the Scriptures. The sickness came from Satan, whose direct responsibility for some sicknesses our Lord distinctly taught. Satan's power is yet undiminished.

Job's sickness was divinely permitted. It was designed to lead him to search his heart and to see his utter need of sanctification.

Job's sickness did not at first sanctify him. It rather led to deeper exhibitions of self-righteousness. Sickness does not purify anyone, although it may lead a person to see his need of holiness and to receive that holiness from God.

Job's sickness was removed when he saw his sin and acknowledged it before God. This revelation came to him from God Himself. Job cried, "Now mine eye seeth thee. Wherefore I abhor myself, and repent in dust and ashes" (Job 42:5–6). Then came his complete justification and with it a spirit of forgiveness and love for others. As he prayed for his friends, the Lord turned his own captivity.

When we become right with God, and as we pray for others, greater blessing will come to us. Job's healing made all things new, and all his blessings were doubled. No doubt the spiritual blessing was the deepest of all.

How instructive to watch Job in the hands of God! Finally he is ready to learn his spiritual lesson and then receive from God's own hand life and restoration.

Israel and the Brazen Serpent

Israel murmured in the wilderness between Egypt and the Promised Land, and God gave Israel something to murmur about. He sent "fiery serpents among the people, . . . and much people of Israel died" (Numbers 21:6). It is a serious thing to complain, for complaining may bring upon us what we fear, or worse. As Job remarked in his affliction, "The thing which I greatly feared is come upon me" (Job 3:25).

Israel's sickness came from Satan—from the serpent. So still he stings our life and poisons our blood. It was a fiery serpent. The Hebrew words are "the serpents, the seraphim." All our spiritual adversaries are not groveling worms. Many of them are lofty and transcendently wise.

The remedy was in the likeness of the disease—a figure of the serpent with the poison extracted. It was a striking intimation to the suffering camp and a sin-stricken world that Satan is robbed of his sting. Sickness and sin are, under the providence of God, mere shadows of their former selves.

There was also in that brazen serpent the thought of Christ made sin for us. Christ assumed the vile and dishonored name of sinful man. Christ was counted by God and treated by men as if He was indeed a serpent and a criminal. Thus for us has He taken the sting from Satan, sin and death. He hung upon the uplifted cross the trophy of victory. "And as Moses lifted up the serpent in the wilderness, even so must the Son of man be lifted up: that whosoever believeth in him should not perish, but have eternal life" (John 3:14–15).

Is it not strange that if medical science is right for the saints, the most striking type of Christ on the cross as shown by Himself is one that was for the healing of the mortal body?

The healing came by looking at the brazen serpent. There is unspeakable power in a look. A look of evil chills the soul. A look of purity and love transfigures it. The eye brings into the soul the object of vision. Looking unto Jesus brings His life into our whole being.

This was physical life. The same life still comes from the risen Christ for spirit, soul and body.

Naaman, the Leper

Naaman's leprosy was a classical instance of disease. Leprosy typified the physical effects of sin, destroying the body. The instrument of his cure was, first, a Hebrew maid. In her helpfulness we learn how God can use a very humble messenger and an incidental word. Indeed, Naaman's own servants, a little later, saved his blessing for him by their wise counsel.

The lesson of humble, obedient faith must next be learned. The proud self-will of Naaman must die before his body can be healed by the divine touch. And so Elisha meets his splendid entourage with quiet independence. He sends him a simple, direct message: wash seven times in the Jordan River and be clean.

The sick are often deeply wounded by God's seeming indifference, but God sometimes thus teaches them the lowliness of faith. He takes their thoughts off themselves and others. Naaman, like all other proud sinners, at first refused the cross. He was about to lose his blessing when a word of honest frankness from his servants brought him to his senses, and he went to the Jordan.

The faith of Naaman consisted in his doing just what the prophet told him. When he took God's way without qualification, and persevered in it, a perfect cure came. Perhaps the first or second or sixth time there was no sign of healing, but he pressed on. At length the wondrous blessing came—flesh like a little child's. Then and there he acknowledged and worshiped the great Jehovah he had found.

His request for a gift of earth from the place of his healing was a beautiful foreshadowing of that greater Gift whom we also receive—the Holy Spirit. Naaman took home with him some of Canaan's soil. We, in our healing, receive the pledge of the Spirit, a part of heaven begun on earth.

It is instructive to see how Elisha sent Naaman away leaning only on God. To his question about bowing in the house of Rimmon, Elisha gave no direct answer. Rather, he threw him on God alone and bade him go in peace. How little man appears in all this and how glorious is God!

King Hezekiah

Hezekiah's was a hopeless case. All men's reasonings about the part the remedy had in curing Hezekiah ought to be set at rest since he was beyond the reach of every remedy. Even God had said that he should die. Man and means could, therefore, have nothing to do with Hezekiah's cure. It was wholly divine.

Hezekiah turned to God in humility. He made no attempt to find help from man. He threw himself helplessly on the mercy of the Lord. His prayer was not a very trustful one, but God heard his cry and sent deliverance.

The answer to his prayer was definite and clear:

15 years more of life from God Himself. It was sent to Isaiah and communicated to Hezekiah by him. Hezekiah at once believed it and began to praise God.

Hezekiah's healing was accompanied by a sign—a reversal of the sundial 10 degrees. Although Isaiah directed a poultice of figs to be applied, both in Second Kings 20 and Isaiah 38 we read that the healing had already been given by God. The poultice was applied on the authority of Isaiah, not on the authority of a "Thus saith the LORD," as in the case of the healing. With all the wealth of detail given in both records, there is no mention of a physician. God has told us to use the anointing oil and the prayer of faith; nothing else is obedience.

The Nobleman's Son

Jesus' healing of the nobleman's son (John 4:46–53) speaks peculiarly to our own times. It teaches us that we do not need the physical and visible presence of our Lord to heal us. Jesus was far from this sick child. He simply spoke a word of power that crossed the intervening space with almighty energy, even as that power still reaches from heaven to earth.

"Oh, if Jesus were only here!" you say. No, this great miracle was performed from a distance. It came about by simple faith without sight or signs. The Lord Jesus led this man away from all but His own word. "Except ye see signs and wonders," He exclaimed, "ye will not believe."

And then He tested the man's faith by a command and a promise: "Go thy way; thy son liveth." The nobleman accepted the hard lesson, believed the naked word and his son was made whole. He showed his faith by quietly returning home, ceasing to clamor for the Lord to visit his son.

This healing began at a fixed moment and developed quietly and gradually, just as so many now are healed. "Then inquired [the nobleman] of [his servants] the hour when he began to amend." The boy was then convalescent. So still the dear Master works for all who trust Him. Faith has both its instants and its hours. We must learn to accept both: to count the death-blow struck at the moment of our believing, and then to follow on as it works out all its stages of blessing.

The Healing of Peter's Mother-in-Law

Christ had just come from the synagogue, where, amid the astonishment of the people, He had cast out a demon (see Mark 1:21ff.). Peter's wife's mother was lying sick of fever. It was a case of ordinary disease. And yet our Lord distinctly recognized another agency behind the fever. "He . . . rebuked the fever," the Bible says (Luke 4:39), and this implies a personal, evil agent causing the fever. Jesus would not rebuke a mere natural law. There is no blame where there is no personal will. Indeed, the fever was the blistering touch of a demon's hand, and this demon was what Jesus rebuked.

Next, Peter's mother-in-law took hold of the healing power which Jesus stood over her to administer. Jesus took her by the hand and lifted her up, and she arose. There was His mighty touch, His almighty help. But there was also the woman's obedience, shown by her receiving His extended hand, and her action in rising. Thus we must meet His help and power.

Then there was the use of her new strength in ministering to Jesus and those with Him. This was the best proof of healing—and the best use of it, too. So must we ever give our new life to God. In ministering to others and forgetting ourselves, we shall find our own strength continually renewed. As we give our lives, we shall save them; as we serve others, Jesus will minister to all our needs.

It is a blessed exchange of responsibility and care to find that we have nothing to do but live for God, while He promises to "supply all [our] need according to his riches in glory by Christ Jesus" (Philippians 4:19). Good health is the richest material blessing of our physical lives. And, as everyone recognizes, it is one of our greatest needs.

The Healing of the Multitude

We read in Matthew 8:16 of a large number of people being healed by Jesus the evening of the Sabbath on which He healed Peter's mother-in-law. They had been gathering all day long, waiting until the Sabbath was past. As soon as sundown came, they pressed upon Him from every side in great numbers. "And [He] healed all that were sick."

Note that they waited until the Sabbath was past. How exactly their prevalent ideas of healing resembled those of our own secular age! They considered the body, and all that pertained to it, to be purely secular. Healing, therefore, was secular work, unfit for the holy Sabbath. Is not this just what modern unbelief has taught the churches of Christendom? The cure of the body is a matter for natural laws and remedies, for secular physicians. It is a profession to be studied and used for profit, like any other business. In no sense is it sacred and holy as is the salvation and culture of the soul.

For the present, our Lord met them on their own ground, but the day soon came when He deliberately healed on the Sabbath day, that He might repudiate this absurd and godless idea and demonstrate that the body was as sacred as the soul. The body's restoration was also part of God's redemption; in no sense was it to be left to mere professional treatment. Jesus considered it to be His own prerogative and business to heal the body. Healing was as holy and sacred a work for the Sabbath as worship at the temple or the salvation of the soul.

Note also the universality of Jesus' healing. He healed all who had need. He wished to show that healing was not for favorite ones such as the mother-in-law of an apostle. Healing was for all sinful, suffering ones who could trust Him.

The highest and most helpful of all the lessons in this episode is the way in which these healings are linked with the prophecy of Isaiah announcing the character of the Messiah as one who would bear our sickness and infirmity. It was with no special and exceptional display of His power as the Son of God that Jesus was healing these sufferers. It was rather the real purpose and design of His Messiahship. And so those in all the ages can come to Jesus and lay upon Him their burdens and their pains.

How deep and full are these words: "Himself took our infirmities, and bare our sicknesses." Himself. Not Himself and physicians, but Himself alone. Not Himself and us, but He takes the whole burden and leaves us utterly free. If Himself, then the healing cannot be had apart from having Him. It is all wrapped up in Jesus—His life in us, His indwelling. "Himself took"—not merely once, but forever—"our infirmities." He not only lifted them once, but He carries them still. Blessed healing! Blessed Healer!

The Man with Leprosy

Soon after the above-mentioned healings, in one of Christ's journeys through Galilee, He healed a man suffering from leprosy. The request of this man—"If thou wilt, thou canst make me clean" (Mark 1:40)—points up the mental attitude of the average Christian. The man had full confidence in the power of Christ to heal, but he was very uncertain about Jesus' willingness.

If a friend is going to doubt me at all, I should much rather he would doubt my ability to help than my willingness. I would rather he said, "I am sure you would help me if you could," than "I know you have it in your power to aid me, but I have little confidence in your disposition to do so." When will we see that this glib talk about God's will involves the most subtle and offensive distrust?

Christ's answer to the man was explicit and emphatic. It ought to settle forever the question of His will to heal the sincere, trusting sufferer: "I will; be thou clean." There is no evasion or ambiguity, no hesitation or conditioning. It is a great, prompt, kingly answer. In it we all may hear His word.

The touch of Jesus meant much to a leper. It was long since a hand of love had touched the man. Jesus' touch was not cold or mechanical. He was "moved with compassion." His heart of love and His very life were in it. Yes, Christ helps us not because His promise compels Him, but because His love overflows toward us.

The cleansed man was to go to the priest at Jerusalem and make a proper acknowledgement and testimony. He was to hold back all other testimony until he had borne witness before the religious authorities of the nation. So we must bear witness of Jesus' mighty works in us. We must do so where He wants us to witness, perhaps in the very hardest place for us and in the very face of religious pride and opposition. For the healed man it was a long journey from Galilee to Jerusalem. If our testimony requires as great a sacrifice for Him, is not His love worth it all?

The Paralyzed Man

In healing the paralyzed man let down through the roof (Mark 2:1–12), our Lord indicated the connection between sin and sickness and assumed the right on earth to forgive sins. And from that moment He was regarded as a blasphemer.

Four of the paralyzed man's friends brought the sufferer for healing, but the Lord saw a deeper need that must first be met. The spiritual life must precede the physical. And so Jesus first speaks the word of pardon: "Son, thy sins be forgiven thee." So we must ever begin. And how many have been led to the very thought of salvation by their need of healing!

Then follows the man's physical healing. But this, too, must be taken by himself in the exercise of bold, obedient faith. He was not healed prostrate on his mat. He must rise, take up his bed and walk. We, too, must arise and step out upon Jesus' strength.

The paralytic was not healed, as is commonly supposed, through the faith of the men who brought him to Jesus, but through his own faith. Their faith laid him at the feet of Jesus and brought to him the word of forgiving mercy. But his own faith had to claim the healing. And it must have been a real faith that could rise up before the throng and carry his bed. The faith of others can do much for us, added to our own, but an unbelieving heart can have nothing from the Lord. (Incidentally, it seems clear from this episode that believers in divine healing should be careful not to assume the responsibility of preventing anyone from seeking medical advice.)

The purpose of healing, as a token of forgiveness and a sign of Christ's saving power, is very solemn. He healed this man that the throng might "know that the Son of man hath power on earth to forgive sins." Christ is ever wanting to convince the world of the reality of His gospel by His physical miracles. How can we expect men to believe that His spiritual gifts are real when we do not permit Him to manifest sufficient power to overcome the physical evils of our life? What right has any man to be sure that any part of his religion is real when his faith has never had enough vigor to accomplish any really difficult thing in his practical life?

The Lame Man at Bethesda

Jesus healed the lame man at the Bethesda pool (John 5:2–9) openly and deliberately on the Sabbath. He purposely intended to refute the idea even then current that disease and the healing arts were secular in nature. He designed to show people that healing was sacred enough to be done on the Sabbath and that it was really an essential part of His spiritual ministry. Many persons are still afraid of unduly exalting the importance of

the body, forgetting that whatever Christ touches
He makes sacred and holy.

The next lesson here has reference to the folly
of the things men depend on for healing. When
the Lord undertook to heal the lame man, He
paid no attention to Bethesda or any other
"means." Rather, He spoke a single word of
power and bade the helpless man go forth in the
strength of God.

There is a lesson, too, for the waiting ones who
are just hoping for some day of help to come.
When Jesus healed the lame man, He dispelled
his dreamy hope of future healing. He started
him on the practical road of present decisions.
Hope is often mistaken for faith. But faith is always in the present. It takes the blessing now.

Another most important lesson is the futility of
leaning on others. "Sir, I have no man . . . to put
me into the pool" expresses the languid dependence of hundreds still. They expect healing
through the help of others. All their own strength
and power through faith in God is paralyzed by
their looking to "means" or to someone else's
faith and prayers. Others cannot help us until we
firmly believe for ourselves. If we cling to others,
our hands only bind and impede them, like the
clinging of a drowning man to his rescuer. Both
may sink together.

Jesus' "Wilt thou be made whole?" expresses
the real element of effectual faith. It acts through
a firm and decided will. Faith is not mere
willpower, but its seat is the will. Will is the

mightiest thing God has given to mankind. No person can receive much from God without making a firm and decided choice. He or she must first see that it is God's will to make whole and then claim that wholeness with uncompromising tenacity.

One more lesson this sufferer must teach us. Jesus warned him, "Sin no more, lest a worse thing come unto thee" (5:14). Not always, yet often, such long and terrible disorders are the direct result of sinful indulgence. Many today are physically powerless because of secret, youthful sins. There must, therefore, be a distinct recognition, confession and repudiation of all sin. And the redeemed life, if it would retain Jesus' sacred life, must be pure and vigilant. But there is no touchstone so searching as the healing life of Christ. There is no cord that binds the soul more sacredly on the altar of holiness than "I am the LORD that healeth thee."

This miracle should not be separated from Jesus' discourse that follows on the life He has come to give. It was just an illustration of that blessed life. Christ's healing is neither more nor less than His own divine life breathed into us, quickening our souls and bodies—beginning eternal life now. This is just what He teaches here: "The Son quickeneth whom he will. . . . The hour is coming, and now is, when the dead shall hear the voice of the Son of God: and they that hear shall live" (5:21, 25).

The Man with the Withered Hand

The healing of the man with the withered hand (Matthew 12:10–13) was a repetition in Galilee of the bold lesson about healing on the Sabbath that Jesus had taught in Jerusalem. In Jerusalem, Jesus healed the powerless man at Bethesda on the Sabbath. Likewise, He healed the man with the withered hand on the Sabbath. Both healings emphasize the same great principle respecting the freedom of the Sabbath, the sanctity of the body and the sacredness of its cure.

They both also teach the same great lesson about the necessity of active and aggressive faith in order to receive Christ's healing power. This man was powerless, too, in his diseased hand. He could not in himself lift it. But he must, nonetheless, put forth an effort of will and an act of force. This he had to do in good faith, really expecting to succeed. And as he did so, the divine power quietly and fully met his obedient act and carried him through into strength and victory.

Thus faith must do things we have no strength to do. As faith is exercised, new strength will come. Just as the priests, in leading Israel across the Jordan River into Canaan, had to step into the water before it parted, so our feet must even touch the cold waters. In passive waiting there can come no life or power from God. We must put our feet on the soil of Canaan, we must stretch forth our hands and partake of the tree of life. "The spider taketh hold with her hands, and is in kings' palaces" (Proverbs 30:28). So many Christians have no grip in their fingers, no stamina in their will, no hold in their faith. Hear Jesus' voice, you who are listless: "Stretch forth thine hand."

In His ensuing arguments with the Pharisees, Jesus leaves no room to doubt the will of God to heal. He ridicules their prejudices against His healing a sufferer on the Sabbath. He declares the healing of this man was an act of simple human compassion—no more than any man would do for an ox or a sheep that had fallen into a pit. Moreoever, it was morally right. To heal is to do good, to save life. Not to heal is to do evil, to destroy life. Certainly Jesus did not treat sickness as a great boon.

Yet such gentle, merciful teaching only exasperated the Pharisees. When they saw God's power vindicate His teachings and the man stand forth before their eyes healed, they were filled with madness. They consulted how they might destroy Jesus. So prejudice still blinds men to the truth and love of God. Still today people oppose Christ's healing ministry because of the hardness of their hearts.

The Woman with a Spirit of Infirmity

Another of Christ's "Sabbath miracles" was the healing of the woman who had a spirit of infirmity (Luke 13:10–20). Because her healing supplements and enforces the same principles of the two other Sabbath healings we looked at, we will introduce it here.

Her disease was a case of helpless paralysis and deformity. She was bowed together and could not lift herself up. She had been 18 years in this condition. She was, therefore, about as difficult a chronic case as could be brought to the great Healer.

The cause of her disease demands special note. Here Jesus throws a ray of marvelously clear light upon the whole question of disease. The Lord distinctly declared that the woman's troubles had come not through natural causes, but through an evil spirit. Her body was bound by "a spirit of infirmity." And Jesus afterward declared that "Satan hath bound [her], lo, these eighteen years." This was not a case of providential discipline but the direct hand of the devil upon the woman's frame.

The question of God's will is also made clear. There is no greater word in Christian ethics than *ought*. It is a word of conscience, of law, of everlasting right. It is a cable that binds both God and man. When God says "ought," there is no appeal, no compromise, no alternative—nothing but an absolute obligation to obey. It does not mean that a thing is possible or permissible or perhaps to be done. It means that it is *necessary* to be done. Not to do it would be wrong.

And Christ said to these evil men who would put their petty prejudices before God's beneficent will and His people's happiness, "Ought not this woman, being a daughter of Abraham, . . . be loosed from this bond?" That should settle the question of how God regards our healing.

But there is one more principle, the greatest of all, and it conditions and limits this "ought" and everything else. It is the woman's faith. The Lord expressly calls her a child of faith, "a daughter of Abraham." The status of the woman makes her healing a matter of "ought." "Ought not this woman, being a daughter of Abraham, . . . be loosed from this bond?" It is the will of God to heal all who believe. More is meant by the expression "a daughter of Abraham" than mere faith. It signifies a very strong faith. Abraham believed without sight and in the face of seeming impossibilities.

Is there evidence of such faith on the woman's part? Yes. We are told that Jesus called her to Him and said, "Woman, thou art loosed from thine infirmity." In the Revised Version it reads, "He called her." It implies that Jesus required her to come to Him first. This would necessitate supernatural exertion and faith. She must have made the attempt to come before He touched her.

Then, as she came, He declared the work done: "Woman, thou art loosed from thine infirmity." He laid His hands on her and completed the work. But her faith had to take the initiative. Like Abraham, she had to step out on the naked word of God. Then the work could be counted done. "Thou art loosed"—and then the full results began to follow.

The Centurion's Servant

In the healing of the centurion's servant (Mat-

thew 8:5–13), we note the high commendation
Christ gave to the faith of a Gentile who possessed little opportunity to know God and enjoy
light. The Bible's most solemn lesson about faith
is that it was most strongly developed in those
who had but little light. Conversely, the greatest
advantages were usually accompanied by the most
unreasonable unbelief.

They who do not promptly use the light they
have are not likely to make a good use of more.
This centurion had very little more light than he
had learned from his own profession and the
smattering of Jewish teaching he may have
gathered. But he had been true as far as he knew
his duty. He had shown his love to God's people
by building them a synagogue at his own expense.

His strong faith showed itself first in his recog-
nizing Christ's absolute control over all the forces
of the universe, even as he controlled his dis-
ciplined soldiers. Second, he recognized the sufficiency of Christ's word to stop the disease. He
asked no more than one word from the Lord of
heaven and earth. That one word he accepted as
final as the decree of the Caesars.

The centurion recognized the authority of
Christ's word. It passes over this universe like a
resistless mandate. Even in the hands of a little
child it is mighty with Christ's own omnipotence.
How tremendous the force of law! Let a single
human voice speak the sentence of the court, and
all the power of wealth and influence are helpless
to hold back the man from a prison cell. The

word that Christ has spoken to us is a word with power. When faith claims it, all the powers of hell and earth dare not resist it. This is the province of faith—to take that imperial word and use its authority against the forces of disease and sin.

The humility of this centurion is a beautiful accompaniment of his faith. He felt deeply his unworthiness of Christ's visit. It was not often that a proud Roman acknowledged himself unworthy of a visit. But this man felt he was standing before One greater than his emperor, and his spirit bowed in lowly reverence and worship.

We can come nearer. Not only will Christ come under our roof, but He will make our heart His home forever.

CHAPTER 6

More Testimonies from Scripture

Let us consider further testimonies to divine healing preserved for us in the Word of God. Like the others, these too bring the gospel of healing down to the personal, applicable level.

The Demented Gadarene

We turn first to the demon-possessed man of Gadara (Mark 5:2–17). There seems no reason to doubt that cases of insanity and diseases of the mind are still the same in character and cause as they were when Christ was on earth. Our Lord distinctly attributed the causes of these disorders to satanic agents. The power that held this man was sufficient to destroy a great herd of swine. What fearful forces one human heart can hold! The power that the evil spirits exerted upon the man's body enabled him to break any chain that the hand of man could place upon him. That gives us some idea of how spirit agents may affect the body either for good or evil.

All physical strength is spiritual in its cause. This wretched man seems to have been conscious of two principles within him. One was his own will, feebly struggling for freedom; the other, the evil spirits controlling him, crushing his will under theirs.

The Lord met this man with deep compassion. He regarded him as the victim of a power he could not resist. By a word of command He set him free. Immediately his whole appearance was changed. The wild and dreaded maniac suddenly was sitting at the feet of Jesus "clothed, and in his right mind."

The extent of the power that had possessed him was soon apparent in the destruction of the swine. He himself clung to his Deliverer and desired to go with Him. But Jesus knew that he needed to be pushed out into the discipline of confession and service. Jesus sent him at once to stand alone and spread the tidings in his home territory. Every new advance would give him new assurance and strength.

Before long the whole region of the Ten Cities was stirred by his testimony. This prepared the way for the Master's visit and a mighty work that closed with the miraculous feeding of 4,000 people. So must we often trust the young disciple with the most bold and difficult service.

The treatment of the insane is one of the most

important questions connected with the subject of faith. The true remedy is the power of Christ. No doubt it is a subject of much difficulty. In many instances there are long and severe trials of faith. But the little that has been attempted has shown how much may be done with holy wisdom and courageous faith.

The Woman Who Touched Jesus' Garment

The healing of the woman who touched Jesus' garment (Luke 8:43–48) is contained within the heart of another: the raising of Jairus' daughter. In these twin miracles the Lord wrote, in one striking lesson, two finely illustrated principles. One was the fact of God's absolute power even to work where there is nothing but death. The other is faith's absolute power to take everything from God.

They emphasize the two wonderful omnipotences that Christ has linked together: "With God all things are possible" and "All things are possible to him that believeth." The helpless nature of the woman's disease and the failure of human physicians are underscored with great plainness of speech. There is no attempt to apologize for the medical profession. We are told frankly that all that had been done for her had only made her worse. Luke, once a physician himself, paints a most vivid picture of all this.

The process of the woman's faith and healing is very striking. There were three stages. First, she believed that she would be healed. She said, "If I may but touch his garment, I shall be whole" (Matthew 9:21). Second, she reached and touched. She did something. The personal and vital element in faith is here brought out very vividly. Faith is more than believing; it is a living contact with a living Savior. It is the outreaching of a conscious need in us, feeling after and finding its supply in God. It is not a mere outward approach, not even a mere mental approach. Hundreds thronged Jesus, but only one touched Him.

Third, the woman consciously received the answer after believing and touching. Immediately her flow of blood was staunched; she felt in her body that she was whole of her plague. She did not feel first and then believe, but she believed and then she felt.

Her blessing, however, had to be confessed. Christ will not allow us to hold His gifts without acknowledgment. We cannot long enjoy and retain them in secret. Like plants, they need the light of day. And so her womanly sensitivity must be laid aside. Her shrinking heart must tell its blessings at Jesus' feet, in the hearing of all. How much we lose by reluctance and silence!

And how much she gained by that confession! Jesus assured her, "Daughter, be of good comfort: thy faith hath made thee whole; go in peace." A daughter, comforted, healed and sent forth into peace. Peace—that deep, divine rest that comes with the touch of God and is the richest part of the inheritance that faith brings.

It is not merely that peace comes into her. She goes into peace—a land so wide and fruitful that she never can know its boundaries or exhaust its precious things. And could one little act of faith for her body bring all this deep spiritual blessing? Yes, the most precious part of the blessing His healing gives is that it heals the whole being. It brings us into union with God with a fullness we never could have known without this living and human touch.

Indeed, most of the great spiritual blessings, experiences and revelations of God to His people in the Scriptures began with what we would call temporal blessings. Abraham became the father of the faithful by believing in God for a son. Jacob became the prince of Israel by claiming a temporal deliverance. Daniel saw the coming of Jesus while asking for the restoration of the captives. The Syro-Phoenician woman won her transcendent victory while pleading for a suffering child. And so still, the things we call little and commonplace are the very pivots on which the greatest spiritual experiences turn. Trusting God for a headache or a dollar may teach us to trust Him for all the fullness of His grace and holiness.

The Two Blind Men

The short story of the healing of two blind men

(Matthew 9:27–31) illustrates several important principles.

Mere prayer will not heal the sick. These blind men followed Jesus from the house of Jairus crying, "Have mercy on us." And yet their petitions brought no reply. "I have been praying for my healing for 40 years," someone occasionally says to me, "and I am no better." Well, little wonder. If the person had prayed in faith, he or she would not have prayed so long.

Mere coming into the presence of Christ will not heal us. They came to Him—into the house—but still they were not healed. So people go to meetings, try to come under spiritual influences and seem to think that these things will bring healing. Perhaps they even present themselves definitely to Jesus for His help and healing, and yet they are no better.

All this is of no avail unless we definitely believe that He does do for us what we claim. "Believe ye?" Jesus asked the blind men, and then He uttered the great law of faith that determines for every one of us the measure of our blessings. "According to your faith be it unto you." Then His touch brought sight and healing, and the men went forth into the glorious light of day.

There is a secret in everything. There is a secret that opens heaven—commands all the forces and resources of the throne. It is not agonizing prayer. It is not much labor. It is simply this: "According to your faith be it unto you."

The Syro-Phoenician Woman's Child

The Syro-Phoenician woman (Matthew 15:21–28) offers us another example of faith when there was little light or opportunity. It is doubtful if this woman in all her life had ever heard a promise of Scripture or seen an inspired teacher. She belonged to an alien race, and everything was against her.

When she came to Jesus, He seemed against her, too. To her pitiful cry for help, He answered her not a word. His disciples appealed to Him to send her away—that is, to grant her request and dismiss her. He replied in language that seemed to exclude her from any right to His mercy. And when at last she came to His very feet and implored His help, He answered in words so apparently harsh and repelling that it seemed like courting insult to approach Him again. He had even called her a dog—in the East a name for the unclean and unfit for fellowship. Yet in the face of all this, the woman's faith only grew stronger until at last she drew out of His very refusal the argument for her blessing.

Difficulties cannot injure true faith. They are the very stimulus of its growth. We see the Lord's design in dealing with us and sometimes seeming to refuse us. All through that struggle Jesus loved the woman and saw the trust that would not be denied. He was only waiting for its full manifestation. Indeed, He tested her faith because He knew it would stand the trial and come forth at last as gold. So He keeps us at His feet and even seems to refuse our cry in order to call forth all the depths of our trust and earnestness.

Another purpose, too, He had for her. He was bringing the woman to the death of self and to a sense of sin. And when at last she was willing to accept His judgment of her and take her place as a worthless sinner—yes, even a "dog," which to her meant the basest of sinners—then she could receive all. Faith is a descent as well as an ascent, a death as well as a life.

The woman's great faith consisted not only in her persistency in holding on but in her ingenuity in finding in His own Word some ground on which to claim the blessing. Faith is a process of logic, an arguing of our case with God. Faith is always looking for something to rest upon. The woman seemed at first to lean upon Jesus' grace and love. She somehow felt it instinctively. Something told her that the One with that calm, gentle face could not refuse her. But still she had no word from Him. Only one little word, one whisper, one faint concession would do. But He had spoken nothing but words of exclusion. And then He spoke the word that seemed to close the door forever. Not only a Gentile, but a dog.

Could she surmount that? But that word became the very bridge on which she crossed. A dog—that gave her a place. Even a dog had some right. She would claim hers.

Only a crumb. The thing she asked for was but a crumb to Jesus, who was so great that mighty deeds of power and love dropped from His fingers. But, oh, it meant so much to her. *Lord, I accept it. I lie down at Thy feet, at Thy children's feet. I ask not their fare, but that which is but their leaving. It will not diminish their share. This I humbly claim for myself and child, and Thou canst not say no.*

Jesus could not say no. Filled with love and wonder, He answered, "O woman, great is thy faith: be it unto thee even as thou wilt." And the mighty deed was done.

"As thou wilt." Here again, we have the same element of decision, of fixed and concentrated will that is essential to all strong faith and action. It was the same determination, in negative form, that overcame at Peniel, 16 centuries before (Genesis 32:24–30). These two instances, both for a temporal deliverance, are companion pictures of overcoming faith.

The Demon-Possessed Child

Immediately after His transfiguration, Jesus was brought face to face with the power of Satan. A demon-possessed child (Mark 9:14–29) had resisted all the efforts of Jesus' disciples. The cause of their failure was a lack of faith. The reason for their unbelief was their contention over personal ambition. When Jesus came to the multitude, He rebuked the unbelief that He perceived and then called the father and child into His presence.

The moment the father began to speak about the difficulties he had had with his son, he fell into an attitude of discouragement. "If thou canst do any thing, have compassion on us, and help us." The Lord's answer quickly brought him to see that it was not a matter of Christ's power, but of his own faith. "If thou canst believe, all things are possible to him that believeth." He at once recognized the tremendous responsibility this placed on him and met it. "Lord, I believe; help thou mine unbelief."

These two words together—the Lord's great word to him and his word to the Lord—are among the most wonderful teachings of the Bible about faith. The first tells us the possibilities of faith—"all things." It signifies God's omnipotence, for the only one to whom all things are possible is God. Faith does, indeed, take and use God's own omnipotence.

The second defines the possibility of faith. It tells us how far we can believe. Many spend their lives wondering if they can believe. Others, like this man, more wisely put forth the effort and then throw themselves on God to sustain them and carry them through.

Had the man said "Lord, help my unbelief" without first saying "Lord, I believe," it would have been vain. Had he said "Lord, I believe" and stopped there, it would have been equally vain, for it would only have been his own willpower. He put forth his will, and then he depended on Christ for the strength. This is faith. It all comes from Christ and is, indeed, His own faith in us. But it must be taken by us and used with a firm and resolute hand.

The healing power now comes, but it seems at first only to make matters worse. There is such desperate resistance from Satan that in the conflict the child is thought by the spectators to be dead. So, often, when God begins to heal us, we really seem to get worse, and the world tells us that we have destroyed ourselves. But death must precede life; demolition, renovation. Let us not fear, but trust Him who knows, and all will be well. Jesus took the child by the hand and lifted him up. The demon had left him forever.

The Blind Man at Bethsaida

The first thing Christ did with the blind man at Bethsaida (Mark 8:22–26) was to take him by the hand and lead him out of the town. He thus separated him from the crowd, giving him time to think. He taught him to walk hand in hand with Himself and to trust Him in the dark. So Jesus first leads us out alone with Himself, long before we look in His face or know that He is leading us.

Next, Jesus began the work of healing the blind man by a simple anointing, as a sign. He put His hands upon his eyes. The result was a partial healing. Sight was distorted and unsatisfactory. Thus would He teach us that sometimes our progress will be partial and by successive stages. Many never get beyond the first stage.

There is a third stage: perfect sight. It comes from one cause: a look at Jesus. "I see men," the man said the first time. And while he saw only men, he saw nothing clearly. But the second time the Lord made him "look up." Then he saw clearly. That one look at Jesus, even through the dimness, made all things clear and whole.

The Blind Man at Jerusalem

The question of sin in connection with sickness receives a very important illumination in the incident of the blind man at Jerusalem (John 9). Christ teaches His disciples that there are cases of infirmity where there has been no special iniquity beyond the common guilt of all men. The trouble has been permitted to afford God opportunity to show His love and power in restoration.

In the healing of this man, the Lord again used a simple sign. He anointed his eyes with saliva and clay. None will say that this could have had any medicinal effect to cure eyes blind from birth. Indeed, it did not cure. It was simply a sign of Jesus' touch. He then sent the man to wash in the pool of Siloam. And he was able to see.

This pool of Siloam was a type of Christ and the Holy Spirit. Siloam, or Shiloh, means the Sent One. The water typified the Holy Spirit, the One sent by the Father and Son.

The subsequent testimony of this man was glorious. With keen sarcasm he exposed the inconsistencies of the Scribes and Pharisees who came to see him. These had hoped to draw out of the man some evidence against Christ, who had again broken the Sabbath by this act of healing. But the humble peasant was more than a match for them, and the controversy that follows is intensely sharp and interesting. Unable to gain their purpose, they at last excommunicated the man from the synagogue. Soon afterward, Jesus appeared to him again and revealed His divine identity. The former blind man became a living disciple.

Blind Bartimaeus

There was a deep insight in the cry of blind Bartimaeus (Luke 18:35–43). "Thou Son of David," he called. Jesus was now coming to claim His throne, and the title by which He was to be known was "The Son of David." It was strange that His own people should be blind to His claim and that a blind man should be the first to see it. So still, the wise are frequently the blind.

We see persistent faith in Bartimaeus. He cried aloud. When people rebuked him, he cried the more. He threw away his garments in his eagerness to get to Jesus. So we must put all hindrances out of the way. Bartimaeus had but one request. His earnest faith summed up all its intensity: "Lord, that I may receive my sight." There can be no strong faith without strong desire. The languid prayer has not motive power enough to ascend to God.

Bartimaeus's healing was simple and glorious. There was a pause, a call, a question, an earnest reply. Jesus spoke the word, the work was done. Bartimaeus gazed on the beautiful scene: the people around him and the face of the Lord.

Looking no farther, he sent up a shout of praise and followed the Lord in the way.

The Withering of the Fig Tree

The cursing of the fig tree (Mark 11:12–14, 20–22) was a miracle of judgment, not a miracle of healing. It would seem to be, therefore, an unpromising theme of faith and comfort. We look at it here because Christ made it the occasion of His highest teaching about faith. It is indeed a symbol of the deepest and tenderest operations of His grace. The greatest principle of Scripture is salvation by destruction, life by death.

The life of the world is the destruction of Satan, sin and death. The sanctification of the soul is the withering up of the natural life. The healing of the body is the death stroke at the root of evil disease. There are things that need God's fire and God's holiness. There are times when we want more than mercy and gentleness, and the spirit longs for the keen sword that slays the foul thing that is crushing life. How glorious at such a time is the consuming holiness of the living God! This is the meaning of the withered fig tree.

"If ye have faith, and doubt not," Jesus told His disciples, "ye shall not only do this which is done to the fig tree, but also if ye shall say unto this mountain, Be thou removed, and be thou cast into the sea; it shall be done" (Matthew 21:21). Yes, we can speak the word of faith, and, the flesh withers and dies. We can speak it again, and the poison tree of sickness is withered. Although leaves and branches may for a while retain their form and color, we know that the death blow has been struck at the root. The real work is done.

The secret is this: "Have faith in God." Literally, "Have the faith of God." The faith *of* God is as different from faith *in* God as Christ's faith is different from that of the disciples who were laboring with the demon-possessed boy. Jesus means to teach us that no less than such a faith as His own will do these things, and we can have it and may take it.

The Lame Man at Gate Beautiful

The first recorded miracle of the Holy Spirit after Christ's ascension was the healing of a lame man begging by the temple gate called Beautiful (Acts 3:1–10). It is marked by the repudiation of all human power or glory and the most emphatic recognition of the name of Jesus only as the source of power. The apostles used that name as their first word to the crippled man. And when the people came crowding around them and the rulers summoned them, they again and again disavowed any personal part in the miracle beyond representing the mighty name and power of Him who had been crucified. He was not then a present but an absent Lord, represented by His ministers invoking His name.

Again, the very faith through which the miracle had been performed and received was as distinctly disavowed as in any sense their own power or the man's. They declared, "Yea, the faith which is by him hath given [the former lame man] this perfect soundness in the presence of you all" (3:16). Both the faith and the power were simply the Lord Jesus Himself working and believing in them.

Again, the miracle was only valued as a testimony for the Lord and an occasion for more widely and effectively spreading His Word. The apostles did not wait to wonder over it. They did not let it monopolize their attention. But they quietly pressed on with their greater work: the preaching of the gospel. The healing of the sick was simply accessory to the great work of the gospel, although it ought always to be associated with it.

The lame man was an unanswerable argument for the gospel, a very buttress in the walls of the young church. "Beholding the man which was healed standing with [the apostles], [the rulers] could say nothing against it" (4:14). We need such testimony still. The world, the infidel and the devil cannot answer them. I have seen the proudest infidel put to shame by a poor woman coming up before the people who knew her and telling how God had made her whole.

Aeneas at Lydda

The healing of Aeneas by the hands of Peter (Acts 9:32–35) has the same features as the healing of the lame man at Gate Beautiful of the temple. Peter is most careful to recognize only the power and name of the Lord. "Aeneas, Jesus

Christ maketh thee whole." Peter is wholly out of sight and ever must be.

The effect of the healing is to bring sinners to God. It is not to set people wondering, but to set them repenting. "All that dwelt at Lydda and Saron saw [the healed Aeneas], and turned to the Lord." The true effect of a gospel of supernatural power is always spiritual. It results in the salvation of men and women. The prophet Joel tells us that through these mighty signs and wonders will come the last great outpouring of the Spirit upon the world and the awakening of men before the Lord's return.

The Lame Man at Lystra

One of the most instructive instances of healing in the Bible is that of the lame man at Lystra (Acts 14:8–10). Lystra was a purely heathen community. The people there had no prejudices. Paul preached "the gospel" to them (14:7). No doubt he told them of the healing and redeeming work of the Lord Jesus.

As Paul preached, he perceived the light of faith and hope irradiating the face of one of his most helpless hearers. God gives the spiritual mind instincts of discernment. He did it for Paul; He does it yet.

Paul evidently would not have gone further unless he had "perceived" that this man had "faith to be healed." It is no use trying to force someone to receive Christ who has not even the desire to do so. It was not Paul's faith that healed the man;

it was the man's faith.

But the man must be helped to act it out. "Stand upright on thy feet," Paul cried. There must be no halting and half-believing. A bold step like this must be carried through audaciously. And lo! the man responded. He not only stood up, but he began to leap and walk. By works, his faith was made perfect.

The effect of the miracle and the self-renouncing spirit of Paul needed no additional word. Paul gave God all the glory, and God was glorified.

Paul's Own Experience of Healing

It was not long until the great apostle had occasion to prove his own faith. The excited people first worshiped Paul and then stoned him. The mob, infuriated by Jewish agitators, dragged him out of the city, and he was left for dead in the midst of the little band of disciples (Acts 14:11–20). But did Paul die? No.

"As the disciples stood round about him, he rose up, and came into the city: and the next day he departed with Barnabas to Derbe"—where he also preached the gospel. Could there be anything more simply sublime or sublimely simple? Not a word of exploitation, no utterance even of surprise, but a quiet trust and deliverance. Then Paul went on about his work in the strength of the Lord.

In Second Corinthians 4, Paul gives us the secret of his strength: "We which live are alway delivered unto death for Jesus' sake"—that was what happened at Lystra—"that the life also of Jesus might be made manifest in our mortal flesh" (4:11). That was the secret of the wondrous restoration at Lystra. Later Paul gives it to us again: "For which cause we faint not; but though our outward man perish, yet the inward man is renewed day by day" (4:16).

In Second Corinthians 1, Paul gives us another instance of his healing. A great trouble came to him in Asia and pressed him above his strength so that he despaired even of life. And, indeed, when he looked at himself, his condition and his feelings, the only answer he could find was death.

But even in that dark hour his confidence was in the resurrection life of Christ and "God which raiseth the dead" (1:9). This trust was not in vain. Christ did deliver him from death. Christ since then had been delivering him. And Paul was sure He would deliver him to the end. Paul simply adds his thanks to the Corinthians for their prayers that had so helped and comforted him. Those prayers gave occasion for wider thanksgiving on his behalf, to the glory of God.

Our Savior's Experience of Physical Life

Our Lord Himself has left to us the great lesson of living physically, not on natural strength and support, but on the life of God. This was the very meaning of His first temptation in the wilderness (Matthew 4:3–4). It was addressed directly to His body. Weakened and worn by abstinence, Jesus heard the tempter suggesting that He should resort to a miracle to supply the means of sustenance and strength. He should make some earthly bread.

The Lord answered that the very reason of His trial and abstinence was to demonstrate that life can be sustained without earthly bread—by the life and Word of God Himself. The words have a deep significance when we remember that they are quoted from Deuteronomy. They were first directed to God's ancient people, to whom God says He had tried to teach this same lesson that "man doth not live by bread only, but by every word that proceedeth out of the mouth of the LORD" (8:3).

So it was not only the Son of Man who was thus to live as a special evidence of God's divine power. The lesson is for every Christian believer. We must all learn to receive our life for the body as well as the soul not by the exclusion of bread, but by God's Word. This is exactly what our Savior meant when, two years later, He said in the synagogue at Capernaum, "As the living Father hath sent me, and I live by the Father: so he that eateth me, even he shall live by me" (John 6:57).

Our Lord refused the devil's bread and overcame in His body for us. The next two temptations were addressed to His soul and His spirit. They were, in like manner, overcome. And so He became for us the Author and Finisher of our faith.

Such are some of the glorious precedents of

faith. In the words of Hebrews 12:1–2, "Seeing we also are compassed about with so great a cloud of witnesses, let us lay aside every weight, and the sin which doth so easily beset us, and let us run with patience the race that is set before us, looking unto Jesus the author and finisher of our faith."

CHAPTER 7

Personal Testimony

All that I know of divine healing and all that I have written in the preceding pages, the Lord Himself had to teach me. I was not permitted to read anything but God's own Word on this subject until long after I had learned to trust Him for myself and, indeed, had written much that is in this book.

For more than 20 years I was a sufferer from many physical infirmities and disabilities. Beginning a life of hard intellectual labor at the age of 14, I broke hopelessly down with nervous exhaustion while preparing for college. For many months I was not permitted by my doctor even to look at a book. During this time I came very near death. On the verge of eternity, I gave myself at last to God.

A Successful Pastor

After my college studies were completed, I became at age 21 the ambitious pastor of a large city church. Plunging headlong into my work, I again broke down with heart trouble and had to go away for months of rest, returning at length, as it seemed to me at the time, to die. Rallying, however, and slowly recovering in part, I labored on for years with the aid of constant remedies and preventives. I carried a bottle of ammonia in my pocket and would have taken a nervous spasm if I had ventured out without it. Again and again, while climbing a slight elevation or going up stairs, an awful and suffocating agony would come over me, and the thought of that bottle as a last resort quieted me.

Well do I remember the day in Europe when I traveled to the top of the Righi in Switzerland by rail, and again when I tried to climb the high Campanile stairs in Florence. As the paroxysm of imminent suffocation swept over me, I resolved never to venture into such peril again. God knows how many hundreds of times in my earlier ministry, when preaching in my pulpit or ministering by a grave, it seemed that I must fall in the midst of the service or drop into that open grave.

Several years later, two other collapses came in my health. They were of long duration. Again and again during those terrible seasons did it seem that the last drops of life were ebbing out.

I struggled through my work most of the time and often was considered a hard and successful minister. But my good people always thought me "delicate." I grew weary of being sympathized with every time they met me. The parishioners excused many a neglected visit because I was "not strong." When at last I took the Lord for my Healer, I asked Him to make me so well that my people would never sympathize with me again. I wanted to be a continual wonder to them through the strength and support of God.

I think the Lord has fulfilled this prayer, for in these recent years they often have been amazed at the work I have been permitted to do in God's name.

It usually took me until Wednesday to get over the effects of the Sunday sermon. About Thursday I was ready to begin to prepare for the next Sunday. Thanks be to God, the first three years after I was healed I preached more than a thousand sermons and held sometimes more than 20 meetings in one week. I do not remember once feeling exhausted.

A few months before I took Christ as my Healer, a prominent physician in New York insisted on speaking to me about my health. He told me that I had not constitutional strength enough to last more than a few months. He required my taking immediate measures for the preservation of my life and usefulness.

During the summer that followed, I went for a time to Saratoga Springs, New York. While there, one Sunday afternoon I wandered out to the Indian campground, where the Jubilee Singers were leading the music in an evangelistic service. I had been deeply depressed. All things in life looked dark and withered. Suddenly I heard the chorus:

> *My Jesus is the Lord of lords:*
> *No man can work like Him.*

Again and again, in the deep bass notes and the higher tones that seemed to soar to heaven, they sang that line:

> *No man can work like Him . . .*
> *No man can work like Him . . .*
> *No man can work like Him.*

The song fell upon me like a spell. It fascinated me. It seemed like a voice from heaven. It possessed my whole being. I took Jesus to be my Lord of lords and to work in my behalf. I knew not how much it all meant. But I took Him in the dark and went forth from that rustic, old-fashioned service, remembering nothing else, but strangely lifted up forevermore.

Old Orchard Beach

A few weeks later I went with my family to Old Orchard Beach, Maine. I went chiefly to enjoy the delightful air of that loveliest of all ocean beaches. I lived on the very seashore while there and went occasionally to the meetings at the campground. But only once or twice did I take part in the services. Up to that time, I had not committed myself in any full sense to the truth or experience of divine healing.

Just the same, I had been much interested in divine healing for a long while. Several years before this I had given myself to the Lord in full consecration, taking Him for my indwelling righteousness. At that time I had been very much impressed by a remarkable case of healing in my own congregation. I had been called to see a dying man given up by all the physicians. I was told that he had not spoken or eaten for days. It was a most aggravated case of paralysis and softening of the brain. So remarkable was his recovery that it was published in the medical journals as one of the marvels of medical science.

His mother was a devoted Christian. The man had been converted in his childhood, but now for many years had been an actor and, his mother feared, a stranger to the Lord. She begged me to pray for him. As I prayed I was led to ask not for his healing but that he might recover long enough to let his mother know that he was saved. I rose from my knees and was about to leave, leaving my prayer where we too often leave our prayers—in oblivion. But some of my people arrived, and I was detained a few minutes introducing them to the mother.

Just then I stepped up to the bed mechanically, and suddenly the young man opened his eyes and began to talk to me. I was astonished and still more so was the dear old mother. And when, as I asked him further, the man gave satisfactory evidence of his simple trust in Jesus, we were all overwhelmed with astonishment and joy.

From that hour he rapidly recovered and lived for years. He called to see me later and told me that he regarded his healing as a miracle of divine power. The impression produced by that incident never left me.

Soon afterward I attempted to take the Lord as my Healer. For a while, as long as I trusted Him, He sustained me wonderfully. But being entirely without instruction and advised by a devout Christian physician that it was presumption, I abandoned my position of simple dependence on God alone and floundered and stumbled for years. But as I heard of isolated cases of miraculous healings, I never dared to doubt them or question that God did sometimes so heal. For myself, however, the truth had no really practical or effectual power, for I never could feel that I had any clear authority in a given case of need to trust myself to God.

I Had to Settle the Matter

In the summer I speak of, I heard a great number of people testify that they had been healed by simply trusting the Word of Christ, just as they would for their salvation. These testimonies drove me to my Bible. I determined that I must settle the matter one way or the other. I am glad I did not go to man. At Jesus' feet, alone, with my Bible open and with no one to help or guide me, I became convinced that this was part of Christ's

glorious gospel for a sinful and suffering world—
the purchase of His blessed cross for all who
would believe and receive His Word.

That was enough. I could not believe this and
then refuse to take it for myself. I felt I dare not
hold any truth in God's Word as a mere theory
or teach to others what I had not personally
proved. And so one Friday afternoon at 3 o'clock,
I went out into the silent pine woods. There I
raised my right hand to heaven and in view of the
judgment day, I made to God, as if I had seen
Him there before me face to face, these three
eternal pledges:

> *1. As I shall meet Thee in that day, I
> solemnly accept this truth as part of Thy Word
> and of the gospel of Christ. Thou helping me, I
> shall never question it until I meet Thee there.*
>
> *2. As I shall meet Thee in that day, I take
> the Lord Jesus as my physical life for all the
> needs of my body until my life work is done.
> Thou helping me, I shall never doubt that
> Thou dost so become my life and strength from
> this moment and wilt keep me under all cir-
> cumstances until Thy blessed coming and until
> all Thy will for me is perfectly fulfilled.*
>
> *3. As I shall meet Thee in that day, I
> solemnly agree to use this blessing for Thy
> glory and the good of others. I agree to speak of
> it or minister in connection with it in any way
> in which Thou mayest call me or others may
> need me in the future.*

I arose. It had only been a few moments, but I knew that something was done. Every fiber of my soul was tingling with a sense of God's presence. I do not know whether my body felt better or not. I did not care to feel it. It was so glorious to believe it simply and to know that henceforth, God had it in hand.

My Faith Was Tested

Then came the test of faith. The first struck me before I had left the spot. A subtle voice whispered, *Now that you have decided to take God as your Healer, it would help if you should just go down to Dr. Cullis' cottage and get him to pray with you.* I listened to the suggestion for a moment without really thinking. Suddenly, a blow seemed to strike my brain that made me reel as a stunned man.

"Lord, what have I done?" I cried. I felt I was in some great peril. In a moment the thought came, *That suggestion would have been all right before this, but you have just settled this matter forever and told God you will never doubt that it is done.* Immediately I understood what faith meant. I understood what a solemn and awful thing it was to keep faith with God. I have often thanked God for that blow. I saw that when a thing was settled with God, it was never to be unsettled. When it was done, it was never to be undone or done over again in any sense that could involve a doubt of the finality of the commitment already made.

In the early days of the work of faith to which God later called me, I was as much helped by a holy fear of doubting God as by any of the joys and raptures of His presence or promises. This little word often shone like a living fire in my Bible: "If any man draw back, my soul shall have no pleasure in him" (Hebrews 10:38). What the enemy desired was to get some element of doubt about the certainty and completeness of the transaction just closed, and God mercifully held me back from it.

The following day I started for the mountains of New Hampshire. The next test came on Sunday, just two days after I had claimed my healing. I was invited to preach in the Congregational church. I felt the Holy Spirit pressing me to give a special testimony. Instead, I tried to preach a good sermon of my own choosing. But it was not the word for that hour, I am sure. God wanted me to tell the people what He had been showing me. Instead, I tried to be conventional and respectable, and I had an awful time. My jaw seemed like lead, and my lips would scarcely move. I finished the sermon as soon as I could and fled into an adjoining field, where I fell to the ground before the Lord and asked Him to show me what He meant and to forgive me. He did—most graciously. And He let me have one more chance to testify for Him and glorify Him.

That night we had a service in our hotel, and I was permitted to speak again. This time I told what God had been doing. Not very much did I say, but I tried to be faithful. I recounted how I had lately seen the Lord Jesus and His blessed gospel in a new way as the Healer of the body. I had taken Him for myself and knew that He would be faithful and sufficient. God did not ask me to testify of my feelings or experiences but of Jesus and His faithfulness. And I am sure He calls all who trust Him to testify before they experience His full blessing. I believe I should have lost my healing if I had waited until I felt it.

I have since known hundreds to fail just at this point. God made me commit myself to Him and His healing covenant before He would fully bless me. I know a dear brother in the ministry, now much used in the gospel and in the gospel of healing, who received a wonderful manifestation of God's power in his body and then went home to his church but said nothing about it. He was waiting to see how it would hold out.

In a few weeks he was worse than ever. When I met him the next time, he wore the most dejected face you could imagine. I told him his error and it all flashed upon him immediately. He went home and gave God the glory for what He had done. In a little while his church was the center of a blessed work of grace and healing that reached far and wide, and he himself was rejoicing in the fullness of Jesus.

I am very sure that Sunday evening testimony did me more good than anybody else. Had I withheld it, I believe I should not be writing the pages of *The Gospel of Healing*.

The Third Test

The next day, the third test came. Nearby was a mountain 3,000 feet high. I was asked to join a small group who were to ascend it. At once I shrank back. Did I not remember the dread of heights that had always overshadowed me? Did I not recall the terror with which I had resolved in Switzerland and Italy never to attempt high places again? Did I not know how ordinary stairs exhausted me and distressed my poor heart?

Then came the solemn, searching thought: *If you refuse to go, it is because you do not believe that God has healed you. If you have taken Him for your strength, need you fear to do anything to which He calls you?*

It was God's thought. I knew my fear would be, in this case, pure unbelief. I told God that in His strength I would go.

I do not wish to imply that we should do things just to show how strong we are or without any real necessity. I do not believe God wants His children needlessly to climb mountains or walk miles just because they are asked to. But in this case—and there are such cases in every experience—I needed to step out and claim my victory sometime, and this was God's time and way. He will call and show each one for himself or herself. And whenever we are shrinking through fear, He likely will call us to the very thing that is necessary for us to do to overcome the fear.

And so I ascended that mountain. At first it

seemed as if it would almost take my last breath. I felt all the old weakness and physical dread. I found I had in myself no more strength than ever. But over against my weakness and suffering I became conscious that there was another Presence. There was a divine strength reaching out to me if I would have it, take it, claim it, hold it and persevere in it.

On one side there seemed to press upon me a weight of death; on the other, an infinite Life. And I became overwhelmed with the one, or uplifted with the other, just as I shrank or pressed forward, just as I feared or trusted. I seemed to walk between them, and the one that I touched possessed me.

The wolf and the Shepherd walked on either side, but the blessed Shepherd did not let me turn away. I pressed closer, closer, closer to His bosom, and every step seemed stronger. When I reached that mountaintop, I seemed to be at the gate of heaven, and the world of weakness and fear was lying at my feet. Thank God, from that time I have had a new heart in this body, literally as well as spiritually, and Christ has been its glorious life.

A few weeks later I returned to my work in New York City. With deep gratitude to God I can truly say, hundreds being my witnesses, that for many years I have been permitted to labor for the dear Lord in summer's heat or winter's cold without interruption, without a single season of protracted rest and with increasing comfort, strength and delight. Life has had for me a zest and labor and exhilaration that I never knew in the freshest days of my childhood.

The Subsequent Years

A few months after my healing, God called me into the special pastoral, evangelistic and literary work that has since engaged my time and energy. I may truthfully say it has involved four times more labor than has any previous period of my life. And yet it has been a continual delight. It has been very much easier in every way than the far lighter tasks of former years.

All the time, however, I have been conscious that I was not using my own natural strength. I would not dare to attempt for a single week on my own constitutional resources what I am now doing. I am intensely conscious, with every breath, that I am drawing my vitality from a directly supernatural source and that it keeps pace with the calls and necessities of my work. Hence, on a day of double labor I will often be aware, at the close, of double vigor and feel just like beginning over again. Indeed, I am almost reluctant to have even sleep place its gentle arrest on the delightful privilege of service. Nor is this a surge of excitement to be followed by a reaction, for the next day comes with equal freshness.

I have noticed that my work is easier and seems to draw less upon my vital energy than before. I do not seem to be using up my own life in the work now, but I am working on a surplus of vitality supplied from another Source. I am sure it is nothing else than "the life . . . of Jesus . . . made manifest in [my] mortal flesh" (2 Corinthians 4:11).

Once or twice since I took the Lord for my strength, I have felt so wondrously well that I began to rejoice and trust in the God-given strength. In a moment I felt it was about to fail me, and the Lord instantly compelled me to look to Him as my continual strength and not depend on the strength He had already given. I have found many other dear friends compelled to learn this lesson and suffer until they fully learned it. It is a life of constant dependence on Christ, physically as well as spiritually.

I know not how to account for this unless it be the imparted life of the dear Lord Jesus in my body. I am surely most unworthy of such an honor and privilege, but I believe He is pleased in His great condescension to unite Himself with our bodies. I am persuaded that His body, which is perfectly human and real, can somehow share its vital elements with our organic life and quicken us from His living heart and indwelling Spirit.

I have learned much from the fact that Samson's physical strength was through "the Spirit of the LORD" (Judges 14:6). Paul declared that although he was daily delivered to death for Jesus' sake, yet the very life of Christ was being made manifest in his body. I find that "the body is . . . for the Lord; and the Lord for the body" (1 Corinthians 6:13). Our "bodies are the members of Christ" (6:15), and "we are members of [Christ's] body, of his flesh, and of his bones" (Ephesians 5:30).

I do not desire to provoke argument, but I give my simple, humble testimony. To me it is very real and very wonderful. I know "it is the Lord." Many of my fellow Christians have entered into the same blessed experience. I only want to consecrate and use this divine life more and more for Him. What a sacred and holy trust it is! I so wish that my weary, broken-down, overladen Christian friends could also taste its exquisite joy and its all-sufficient strength.

To my brothers in the ministry I would like to add that I have found the same divine help for my mind and brain as for my body. Having much writing and speaking to do, I have given my pen and my tongue to Christ to possess and use. God has so helped me that my literary work has never been a labor. He has enabled me to think much more rapidly and to accomplish much more work and with greater facility than ever before. It is very simple and humble work; but such as it is, it is all *through* Him and, I trust, *for* Him only.

With all its simplicity, I believe it has been more used to help His children and glorify His name than all the elaborate preparation and toil of the weary years that went before. To God be all the praise!

CHAPTER
8

Testimony of the Work

Let me add a few words about the beginning of the ministry of divine healing in New York City and some of the instances that I have known.

As I have already stated in the previous chapter, one of the pledges I made to the Lord concerning my own healing was that I would use this truth and my experience of it for the good of others as He should require and lead me.

This was no small thing for me. I had a large amount of conservative respectability. I had high regard for my ecclesiastical reputation. I knew intuitively what it might cost to be wholly true in this matter. At the same time, I shrank unutterably from the thought of having to pray with anyone else for healing. I feared greatly that I should involve God's name in dishonor by claiming what might not come to pass. I almost hoped that I might not have to minister personally in this matter. I was intensely glad that God had already raised up other ministers for this work, and I would gladly strengthen their hands.

My first public testimony in New York to the truth of divine healing, made in the course of a sermon to my own people, then a Presbyterian church, awakened little or no opposition. A few weeks later I was asked to speak at the anniversary of the Fulton Street Prayer Meeting—the day of President James Garfield's funeral. The Lord led me to speak frankly and refer to the true scriptural method of prayer for the direct healing of the sick in the name of the Lord Jesus. At the close of my address there was only one who gave me a word of response. He was a Methodist presiding elder. He thanked me very cordially and said he believed every word I had said.

A Family Crisis

Soon after, a test came in my own family. My little daughter became suddenly very ill with diphtheria. Her mother, not then believing at all as I did, insisted upon having a physician. She was much distressed when I simply took the little one to God and claimed her healing in the name of the Lord Jesus. That night, with a throat as white as snow and a raging fever, the little sufferer lay beside me alone. I knew that if the sickness lasted until the following day, there would be a crisis in my family and I should be held responsible.

The dear Lord knew it, too. With trembling hand I anointed her brow. She was the first or second person I had ever anointed. I claimed the power of Jesus' name. About midnight my heart was deeply burdened. I cried to God for speedy deliverance.

By morning my daughter was well. I shall never forget the look my wife gave me when she saw the ulcers gone and our child ready to get up and play.

About that time the Lord led me to commence the special work of faith that has since engaged my life. This was not by any means to teach divine healing but to preach the gospel to the neglected masses by public evangelistic services. For several years no single word about physical healing was spoken in those meetings, our supreme object being to lead men and women to Christ and not to prejudice them by any side issues.

But the facts about my own healing and the healing of my child spread quietly among my little flock. One and another came to me to ask about it and whether they could be healed also. I told them they could if they would believe, as I had done, and I sent them to their homes to read God's Word for themselves and to ponder and to pray.

The first inquirer was a dear sister, then widely known in Christian work, who afterward became a deaconess in our Berachah Home. She had suffered from heart disease for 20 years. She took about a month to weigh the matter. Then in her calm, decided way she came to have her case presented to God. Instantly she was healed. For several years she worked untiringly, hardly knowing what weariness even meant. At length she finished her work and fell asleep amid great peace and blessing.

Others began to come and ask about physical healing. At length the Friday meeting grew up as a time and place where all who were interested in this special theme could gather, be instructed and strengthen each other by mutual testimony. This meeting has since grown in size to several hundred people from all the evangelical churches and many different homes.

The Blessing Is for All

The cases of healing that have come under my notice in these years would fill many volumes. They have represented all social extremes, all religious opinions, all professions and callings and all classes of disease. I have had spiritists come, broken down at length by the service of Satan and seeking deliverance from their sufferings. I have never felt free even to pray with such without a complete renunciation of this snare.

I have had Roman Catholics come as if they were consulting some oracle. And when they have been patiently instructed and led to the true Savior, I have seen them healed. I have had men come and offer large sums if they or their dear ones could be prayed back to health. I have never dared to touch such cases except to send them directly to Christ and tell them that at His feet only, in true penitence and trust, could they expect deliverance.

I have had poor sinners come seeking healing and go having found salvation. Many people have been led to Christ through their desire to escape disease. I have never felt that I could claim the healing of anyone until he or she first accepted Jesus as Savior. But I have several times seen the soul saved and the body healed in the same hour.

I have never allowed anyone to look to me as a healer. I have had no liberty to pray for others while they placed the least trust in either me or my prayers—or in anything or anyone but the merits, promises and intercessions of Christ alone. My most important work has usually been to take myself and my shadow out of people's way and set Jesus fully in their view.

I have seen very humble and illiterate Christians suddenly and gloriously healed and baptized with the most wonderful faith. I have seen intellectuals and Christians who had great reputations unable to touch even the border of Christ's garment. I saw a brilliant physician once rise in the meeting and make a learned speech about healing. And I saw a humble girl who, when I first met her, did not seem to have capacity enough to grasp the idea, healed by His side of the worst stage of tuberculosis and her shortened limb lengthened two inches in a moment.

I have seen this blessed gift of Christ bring relief and unspeakable blessing to the homes of many of the poor. I have seen it take from worn and weary working women a bondage like Egypt's iron furnace. And I have also seen it enter the homes of many of the refined, the cultivated and the wealthy who have not been ashamed to witness a good confession and bear a noble testimony to Christ as a complete Savior.

I have seen the theologian often answered after his most logical assaults upon it by the healing of some of his own people in a way he could not answer or explain. Sometimes I have taken one of these simple persons to a boasting infidel and asked him or her to testify to the person concerning what God has done. I have seen infidels overwhelmed, silenced and sometimes deeply impressed.

Often have I seen women of the world break under deep conviction of sin and seek a true and devout religious life by the simple, genuine testimonies of the Friday meeting. I have seen many a clergyman accept the Lord Jesus in His fullness for soul and body. Some of the most devoted and distinguished servants of Christ are glad to own Him as their Healer. But I have also noticed that the ecclesiastical straitjacket is the hardest fetter of all, and the fear of man the most inexorable of all bondages.

Not a few physicians of the highest standing have taken Jesus as their Healer, and when their patients are prepared for it, they love to lead them to Christ's care. Many of the most consecrated Christian workers and city missionaries have found this precious truth. Some have faced a bitter ordeal of prejudice and opposition in their churches and organizations. But when they have been wise, true and faithful, God has vindicated them in the end.

I have found that the most spiritually minded men and women in the various churches are usually led to see and receive this truth. When Christ becomes an indwelling and personal reality in the soul, it is hard to keep Him out of the body.

What about Medical Remedies?

I have not found any serious practical difficulty in dealing with the question of remedies. Where a person sets any value on them or is not clearly led of the Lord to abandon them, I never have advised him or her to do so. There is no use in giving up remedies without a real personal faith in Christ. And when a person really commits his or her case to Christ and believes that Christ has undertaken, he or she does not want, as a rule, any other hand to touch it. He or she does not see that anything else is necessary.

Where people have real faith in Christ's supernatural help, they will not want remedies. And where they have not this faith, I have never dared to hinder them from having the best help they can obtain. I have never felt called to urge anyone to accept divine healing. I have found it better to present the truth and let God lead them. Often when urging them most strongly not to attempt it unless they were fully persuaded, the effect has been to impel them to it more strongly and to show that they had real faith. I have never felt that divine healing should be regarded as the gospel. It is part of it, but we labor much more assiduously for the salvation and sanctification of the souls of men and women.

The cases of healing have been varied. One of the most remarkable in the early days was a woman who had not bent her joints for eight years. She used to stand in our meetings on her crutches, unable to sit down during the whole service. She had not sat for eight years. She was healed in a moment, and all in the house were filled with wonder.

Another was cured of spinal curvature. A great many have been delivered from fibroid tumors and a few from malignant and incurable cancers. We have seen broken bones restored without surgical aid. We have seen God heal severe heart disease, tuberculosis and hernia, when it would have been death to walk forth as they did if Christ had not sustained. Paralysis and softening of the brain, epilepsy and St. Vitus' dance—even a few cases of dangerous insanity—all have been markedly cured through believing prayer. The numbers of such healings will reach to thousands.

Consecrated Lives Our Chief Joy

Our chief joy has been in the consecrated lives thus redeemed from destruction and given to the work of God and the needs of mankind. These are blessed and glorious. One person is in charge of a mission where hundreds are led to Christ. Another, refused by her mission board on account of illness, was healed by the Lord and is again in India with her husband, preaching Christ. Some are in Japan, some in Africa, some in South America, some in England. Many are in the streets and lanes of New York City and in the most earnest work of our land. God be thanked for the blessings they have received, and the blessing they have become.

During these years the Lord has opened our Berachah Home and allowed us to meet hundreds of His dear children within its walls. We have seen them go forth in strength and blessing. Other homes of healing are scattered over this and other lands. Already a great multitude are joining hands and singing together these verses from Psalm 103 as they journey home:

> *Bless the LORD, O my soul: and all that is within me, bless his holy name. Bless the LORD, O my soul, and forget not all his benefits: who forgiveth all thine iniquities; who healeth all thy diseases; who redeemeth thy life from destruction; who crowneth thee with lovingkindness and tender mercies; who satisfieth thy mouth with good things; so that thy youth is renewed like the eagle's.*

Abiding and Confiding

I am crucified with Jesus,
And He lives and dwells with me;

I have ceased from all my struggling,
'Tis no longer I, but He.
All my will is yielding to Him,
And His Spirit reigns within;
And His precious blood each moment
Keeps me cleansed and free from sin.

All my sicknesses I bring Him,
And He bears them all away;
All my fears and griefs I tell Him,
All my cares from day to day.
All my strength I draw from Jesus,
By His breath I live and move;
E'en His very mind He gives me,
And His faith, and life, and love.

For my words I take His wisdom,
For my works His Spirit's power;
For my ways His ceaseless presence
Guards and guides me every hour.
Of my heart, He is the portion,
Of my joy the boundless Spring;
Saviour, Sanctifier, Healer,
Glorious Lord, and coming King.
—A. B. Simpson

Books about A.B. Simpson

All for Jesus (History of The Christian and Missionary Alliance), by Robert Niklaus, et al.
The Baptism of the Holy Spirit: The Views of A.B. Simpson and His Contemporaries, by Richard Gilbertson
Body and Soul: Evangelism and the Social Concern of A.B. Simpson, by Daniel J. Evearitt

Books by A.B. Simpson

Best of A.B. Simpson (compiled by Keith M. Bailey)
Christ in the Bible Commentary—Six Volumes
Christ in the Tabernacle
Christ in You
The Christ of the Forty Days
Cross of Christ
Danger Lines in the Deeper Life
Days of Heaven on Earth (devotional)
Divine Emblems
The Fourfold Gospel
The Gentle Love of the Holy Spirit
The Gospel of Healing
The Holy Spirit—Power From on High
The Land of Promise
A Larger Christian Life
The Life of Prayer
The Lord for the Body
Loving as Jesus Loves
Missionary Messages
The Names of Jesus
Portraits of the Spirit-Filled Personality
Practical Christianity
Seeing the Invisible
Serving for the King

The Spirit-Filled Church in Action
The Supernatural
Walking in Love
When God Steps In
When the Comforter Came
Wholly Sanctified
The Word Made Flesh (commentary on the *Gospel of John*)

Booklets by A.B. Simpson

A.W. Tozer and A.B. Simpson on Spiritual Warfare
Christ Our Sanctifier: A.B. Simpson on the Deeper Life
Gifts and Grace
Hard Places: Stepping Stones to Spiritual Growth
Higher and Deeper: A Roadmap for Christian Maturity
Himself
Is Life Worth Living? A Study in Ecclesiastes
Paul: Ideal Man, Model Missionary
Thirty-One Kings: Victory Over Self